A Useful Guide to Observing
Schools in Action

# Looking Behind the Classroom Door

John I. Goodlad
M. Frances Klein
and Associates:

Cynthiana E. Brown
Edith B. Buchanan
Janet R. Harkness
Madeline C. Hunter
Dorothy M. Lloyd
Jimmy E. Nations
June Patterson
Billy R. Plaster
Clara G. Rodney
Robert L. Sinclair
Louise L. Tyler

Charles A. Jones Publishing Company
Worthington, Ohio

1  2  3  4  5  6  7  8  9  10  /  78  77  76  75  74

Library of Congress Catalog Card Number: 72-85802

International Standard Book Numbers: 0-8396-0036-4   paper
                                     0-8396-0035-6   cloth

Printed in the United States of America

# Preface

*Looking Behind the Classroom Door* provides a necessary beginning point from which to work toward continuous self-renewal in schools. The book gives the reader useful information about innovations, expectations, and problems of reconstructing schooling; detailed descriptions of what actually goes on in schools and classrooms today; and an extensive instrument for the systematic observation of schools in action for looking behind school and classroom doors.

It is essential that educational change begin from a full understanding of what already exists. An analysis of many efforts to improve schools, particularly the curriculum, in recent years reveals that proposals often emerged out of whole cloth without knowledge of the shape of schooling and the raiment most likely to be required or welcomed. Consequently, the proposed changes did not fit or were not readily received or both. Change was blunted on school and classroom door.

In many ways, the school is a self-contained social system with its own unique ways of functioning: expectations which are reasonably well understood and accepted by those who come to school each day; rather clearly defined roles for students, teachers, and administrators; activities through which these roles are fulfilled; and relatively clear reward systems. Suggested changes appearing to upset these expectations, roles, activities, and rewards often are threatening. However well-meaning and desirable the proposals may be, the net effect is to close the system more tightly into itself instead of opening it up so as to be responsive to change. Failure to understand the social system of the school, then, is to prejudice at the outset the chances for success of any innovation. This is particularly the case for change agents outside the school but applies also to those seeking change from within.

It is the thesis of this volume that all who are involved or to be involved in schools should be students of schools. The first edition

*iii*

emphasized what goes on day by day in a sample of 67 schools in the United States, drawing from a massive quantity of observational data. This edition provides this same body of data but has been revised to turn attention to the *process* of observing life in schools. There is a subtle shift in orientation from prior concern with reporting our observations to encouraging observation by others: teams of pre-service or in-service teachers, educators concerned with change and innovation, and researchers. This shift includes concern for how schools might be reconstructed (Chapter Five).

The close-range view of school practices, as explored in the previous edition of *Behind the Classroom Door,* leads us to three critical entry points for improving schooling. The first pertains to the pedagogical skills acquired by future teachers in training. The second is the updating of these skills on the job. And the third is the continuous reconstruction of schooling to meet the changing conditions of communities and of society in general.

Chapter One summarizes some of the organizational, curricular, and instructional thrusts which have been widely recommended for our schools and which one might reasonably expect to be substantially implemented there. Chapter Two describes the procedures of data collection and analysis for the observational study presented here. Chapter Three summarizes the wealth of material from these raw data and Chapter Four sets forth some conclusions and generalizations about schools and classrooms, with the expectations of Chapter One as points of reference. We set forth in Chapter Five some further insights into the conduct and structure of schooling in the United States, particularly as evidenced in a five-year study of educational change.

The two-part Instrument for Study of Childhood Schooling in the Appendix will help those wanting to improve their knowledge and consequent understanding of teaching practices to assure the full development of human potential. It includes not only the categories and items used in our observations but also some minor revisions and, in addition, examples of readings which might be consulted to improve understanding in the several areas of school and classroom practice. This guide to references is deliberately incomplete; instructors and students in education courses will want to flesh out the framework with their own readings.

There is a growing interest in this country and abroad (India, Iran, Israel, Korea, the Netherlands, Norway, and Sweden to identify a few examples of other countries) in finding out the state of the field regarding the conduct of schooling, as a first but often overlooked step in projecting plans for needed reform in curriculum, instruction, and teacher education. Our observation guide might provide at least a beginning for researchers seeking to develop an instrument appropriate to their purposes of description and analysis.

Schooling in the United States can and must be revitalized. This cannot be done, however, by adding an innovation here or there. Systematic conceptualizations of what is required followed by systematic, step-by-step reconstruction are called for. The major educational challenge of our time is to reform our existing schools and school systems. This is our educational mandate for the 1970s.

John I. Goodlad

University of California, Los Angeles
and
Institute for Development of Educational Activities, Inc.

M. Frances Klein

University of California, Los Angeles
and
Educational Inquiry, Inc.

# Acknowledgments

*Associates* for this work are those persons who either gathered data or assisted in its analysis: Cynthiana E. Brown, Edith B. Buchanan, Janet R. Harkness, Madeline C. Hunter, Dorothy M. Lloyd, Jimmy E. Nations, June Patterson, Billy R. Plaster, and Robert L. Sinclair are or were members of the faculty, University Elementary School; Clara G. Rodney is on the faculty of California State College, Long Beach; and Louise L. Tyler is a professor at the University of California, Los Angeles.

*Collaborators* assisted in a variety of ways: Sara N. Breit, Margaret J. Brown, Mary Nelson Campbell, Enid E. Fremdling, and Barbara Johnson, all of the U.E.S. staff, assisted in conceptualizing the project and testing anecdotal procedures; Gerda Lawrence, also of the staff, provided training in interview techniques; William L. Duff, University of Northern Colorado, Greeley, assisted in analyzing and summarizing the data; Virgil M. Howes, International Center for Educational Development, Los Angeles, provided helpful counsel at various stages as the project progressed; Mary Louise Bell, Arline Duff, Ann Edwards, Elizabeth Howard, Corann Pesqueira—then associated with the University Elementary School—and Elisabeth Tietz of the Institute for Development of Educational Activities, Inc., were responsible for scheduling, correspondence, and like matters for this insightful work.

We are grateful to those who are acknowledged and many more who assisted us in various ways. Funds for this study were provided by the Ford Foundation. We thank Edward J. Meade, Jr., of the Foundation for his support and encouragement and, most of all, for his unquestioning belief in us.

Madeline C. Hunter, principal of the University Elementary School, UCLA, merits special recognition. Because of her administrative skill, it was possible to deprive the school of key teachers from time to time without impairing any of the many functions served by it. Also, we thank Lillian K. Drag for bibliographic additions to the observation guide included in this book.

# Contents

# Chapter One

# Expectations in Observing
# Childhood Schooling

The winds of educational change blow strong today in America. For more than a decade, great cumulonimbus clouds of educational reform have been blowing back and forth across the United States. To what extent have these clouds nourished with their fresh moisture the fields below? Succeeding pages seek to provide both the answer to this question and some hypotheses regarding what is required to improve schooling in areas of recognized weakness.

The nature and requirements of schools and school systems in the United States have been the focus for study, debate, and action throughout this century. A particularly strong drive for educational reform took place during what might be called the education decade, beginning in 1957 and concluding about 1967. A unique feature of this period was that federal leadership saw education as vital to the nation's strength and well-being and committed itself to support at the very time that leading laymen and educators sensed a need for change at all levels of the educational system. The launching of the Soviet satellite Sputnik symbolized for many our educational deficiencies and stimulated both funds and ideas for reform.

*3*

Shortly after World War II, a strong reaction had set in against "progressive" educational practices which were perceived as having been dominant for decades. Military testing programs had revealed disturbing inadequacies among high school graduates in such fields as mathematics, foreign languages, and the natural sciences — inadequacies which were attributed in large measure to the assumed excesses of progressive education. The resulting attack on progressive education reached peak proportions in 1951. But it was Sputnik, six years later, that aroused the public to widespread concern about their schools. Meanwhile, the clouds of reform were already gathering.

Proposals for change were in three classic realms of schooling: curriculum, organization, and instruction. Updating and reorganization of the mathematics curriculum got well underway in the early 1950's. Reform in the natural sciences and foreign languages soon followed, all at the secondary-school level. Change in the social sciences and humanities came more slowly, as did proposals for improvement at the elementary-school level. At the heart of almost all curriculum reform projects was the idea that separate subjects, rather than combinations of subjects, should prevail, with emphasis on the structural methods and elements of each discipline. A second major idea was that students should be encouraged to inquire for themselves into the subject matter, discovering this structure and the excitement of discovery in the same way that the scientist does.

At the outset, teachers who were to use the new curriculum materials were carefully introduced to these ideas through summer and year-long institutes. With the passage of time, however, in-service teacher education received less attention. At no point was there intensive attention to the re-education of elementary-school teachers.

Proposals for reorganizing the schools drew heavily from increasing knowledge about individual differences among students and recognized the fact that rapid expansion in knowledge placed undue burdens on elementary-school teachers attempting to teach all subjects. The nongraded school was proposed as a plan for taking account of the enormous range of ability and attainment in a class group. Team teaching was introduced as a way for teachers to share the complex processes of teaching by pooling strengths and including *para*professionals, aides, and student teachers in the instructional effort.

Recognition of individual differences and concern for individualized progress also characterized recommendations for instructional improvement. A technique named programmed instruction was designed for the purpose of enabling each student to proceed at his own pace through the stages or steps of a sequence of learning. These programs were designed for presentation in textbooks, on individually-operated teaching machines, or by computers.

Throughout, there was great interest in how to develop independent, self-directed learners, an interest which has found voice in the educational rhetoric since the turn of the century. In fact, most of the ideas surging to the forefront during the so-called education decade were not new, although they may have appeared in new dress. Many have been at the core of proposals for changing the schools for many decades and have been brought to the attention of teachers through books, education courses, conventions, workshops, and institutes. The need for stimulating subject matter, a diversity of instructional materials, individualization of learning and teaching, student involvement in planning his learning, learning how to learn, and so on are well-worn pedagogical ideas receiving widespread teacher endorsement. One would expect them to be rather well established in school practice.

Events of the time and certain experiences of our staff*
led us to wonder, however, whether some of our most widely
recommended and, presumably, accepted educational ideas
have found their way into the classrooms. We became interested in finding out what actually goes on behind school and
classroom doors, especially with respect to those most frequently recommended changes. We were particularly interested in the child's early school experience in the primary
years, beginning with kindergarten.

## Early Education Practices

Our interest was heightening at the very time the importance and possibilities of preschool education were receiving
national attention. The Israeli experience in providing schooling for immigrant four-year-olds was widely cited and discussed.[1]** Montessori schools, enrolling nursery school age as
well as older children, increased in number across the United
States. The National Laboratory on Early Childhood Education, with several university-based centers, was established to
collate and conduct research, develop model programs, train
personnel, and disseminate findings and information. Simultaneously, the Educational Policies Commission of the
National Education Association proposed the nationwide expansion of public schooling to embrace, first, four-year-olds of

---

*Our staff refers to the teachers and administrators of the University
Elementary School, UCLA, and especially to those who participated
most actively in the inquiry explored here. We set out to satisfy our
curiosity and hope that we have aroused yours enough to join with us
in this analysis of where that curiosity led us.
**References appear in numbered sequence at the end of each chapter.

culturally disadvantaged groups and, as soon as possible thereafter, all four-year-olds. And, at the beginning of the decade, Jerome S. Bruner gave us the statement most often quoted as justification for the downward extension of early, formal education for the young: ". . . any subject can be taught effectively in some intellectually honest form to any child at any stage of development."[2]

The rhetoric expressing this heightened interest in early education has stressed "preschool"; that is, a period of formal schooling immediately preceding children's entry into the existing school system, an entry which occurs for almost all children between the ages of five and seven. This rhetoric has implied, more by connotation than explication, downward extension of at least the most rudimentary elements of first-grade instruction, particularly the vocabulary development considered basic to reading. Most program development has been motivated by and directed to the special problems of children in the harsh, inner sectors of our cities — children whose environmental circumstances are believed to handicap them severely in their later encounters with school.

"Preschool" suggests a period of preparation for the real thing which is to follow. Looking at these programs, our staff feared that the main race might not be appropriate for many of the children who inevitably would run it and that, consequently, early trials on the track might be as detrimental for some as no trials at all. It seemed to us that the early education of young children, whether or not environmentally disadvantaged, should be guided more by principles of learning and development than by existing models of primary schooling. School, we believed, has certain built-in institutional rigidities which do not respond readily to new insights and proposals for change. New programs for age groups not encompassed by school provide, then, a unique opportunity to

7

be guided by educational reasons rather than by institutional habits.

In brief, we feared that "crash-type" educational programs for the young would tend to model themselves after school practices which do not reflect the best use of such practical educational wisdom as is available. Earlier visits to schools had raised serious questions about extending schooling practices downward in wholesale fashion, in spite of widespread talk of change and innovation.[3] Further, Martin Mayer's conclusions, based on thirty months of observing, interviewing, and reading, while sometimes optimistic, included the telling comment: "The higher one's view of human potential, the more one will dislike the schools as they actually exist."[4] Paul Goodman was less kind in suggesting ". . . that perhaps we already have too much formal schooling and that, under present conditions, the more we get, the less education we will get."[5] Their books and articles were forerunners to a raft of critical successors which included the biting and often hilarious *Up the Down Staircase* and such doleful titles as *The Tyranny of Schooling, Robots in the Classrooms,* and *Our Children Are Dying.*[6]

Our conversations with teachers, principals, and superintendents who visit our school — 3500 to 5000 in any given year — both puzzled us and increased our curiosity about elementary-school practices. Although certain rather widely recommended practices, particularly those pertaining to the individualization of instruction, had become standard procedure with us, they clearly were viewed as innovative by our visitors. Had this not been the case, of course, they probably would not have visited. But what so often caught us by surprise was evidence that no ongoing structures for changing existing practices seemed to exist in many—in fact, in most—of the home settings.

Many of these visitors were quite uncertain as to how proposals for change would be received in their local school systems. Others indirectly provided evidence that regular faculty meetings to discuss anything other than routine matters simply did not take place in their schools. Clearly, for most, change was not just a matter of carrying home new ideas. There was need to create both a responsiveness and a structure conducive to the rational updating of school practices.

Teachers, principals, and superintendents often appeared to be almost starved for intellectual stimulation. They wanted help, frequently at the most basic levels of getting started. Invitations to serve as innovating middlemen in school systems, schools, and classrooms had to be politely declined. Increasingly, questions of earlier years pertaining to "why are you doing it?" were being replaced by "how do you do it?" The perspective required for dealing effectively with such questions required knowing more about the settings in which our visitors worked and for which our answers were to take on meaning. And this, we concluded, necessitated firsthand observation.

## Some Values for Childhood Schooling

Through firsthand observation, experience, reading, and intensive discussion, our staff has been strengthened in the belief that there are certain pedagogical concepts or principles which are generally applicable in childhood schooling, if one takes time to study the prime subject matter. But this subject matter is *children* — not reading, writing, and arithmetic.

*We believe that the best hope for a self-renewing society is a self-renewing individual who has been provided with every possible opportunity to develop his unique talents and capa-bilities.* If schools are to contribute significantly to the development of such a society and such an individual, they must search out, approve, and foster many attributes which, in the past, have been excluded from school scope. To us, this means that children are teachers' prime data. Teachers must be engaged continuously in a process of diagnosis to determine not just whether the *level* of work is appropriate for the child but whether there might be, for him, better work.

*We believe that the development of rational powers is the good work for which education is admirably suited and uniquely responsible.* Rationality involves much more than cognitive acuity. It involves the acquisition of knowledge, the careful weighing and appraising of that knowledge, the consideration of alternatives, the formulation of convictions and action based on such convictions.[8] If rationality is something that can be taught, teaching must assure much more than the regurgitation of information. The "press" of school and classroom should carry the child far beyond mere storage and recall of information to applications, evaluations, doubt, and the search for new meanings and new ways of behaving.

*The educated man is fully aware of societal restraints, the reasons for them, and their appropriateness or inappropriateness for mankind.* But he does not need to be policed, coerced, or threatened in order to behave responsibly. In fact, the greater the restrictions to his freedom of thought and action, the less his opportunity to learn and to exercise responsible behavior — in effect the less his opportunity to become educated. Consequently, school and classroom should emphasize, from the very earliest years, opportunities for each child to assume responsibility for his own behavior. Each must be permitted to make mistakes, to suffer the consequences of actions, and to run the risk of incurring displeasure on the part of classmates. The process of becoming self-disciplining is a slow, painful one. Teachers must resist the temptations both to assume responsibility for the child and to make what can be only false progress through the application of temporary, external control.

*The most useful learning is to have learned how to learn.* Part of this learning lies in understanding both principles linking phenomena and that there are such principles. Most of the rest is in acquiring tools and processes ranging from reading skills to modes of thinking about or inquiring into the widest possible array of human and physical phenomena. The school must eschew, then, the deceptively easy temptation to teach a rhetoric of conclusions.[9]

*Education is a lifelong process in which schooling plays a decreasingly significant role.* Everything about the conduct of school should emphasize its temporary, dispensable character.[10] Teachers, consequently, must underplay their role as sources of intellectual authority by involving their pupils in inquiry into the idea that knowledge is neither fixed nor immutable. Ideally, the child develops a sense of personal power by participating productively in educational adventure.

*There are many roads to learning.* It is extremely unlikely that any best one will be discovered. Rather there are likely to be better or worse ways for certain children under certain conditions. Therefore, it seems desirable for school and classroom to open up many possibilities, to provide always a range of alternatives. It is particularly important for the young child to explore many learning styles before settling on those likely to characterize later behavior. Teachers must resist the temptation to impose their own idiosyncratic learning styles or those methods which characterized their own favorite teachers.

These statements provide at least a preliminary set of values for viewing educational practice. They constitute our biases, too, and should be made explicit here so that there is full awareness of beliefs which, no doubt, influenced our perceptions of school practices and, in fact, any data secured. Even observers of natural phenomena, claiming objectivity, cannot escape their colored glasses.

## Ten Reasonable Expectations

Returning now to educational change, many of the ideas guiding recent proposals for educational reform are not new. Our interest was in finding out the degree to which frequently discussed ideas for schooling prevail in practice. We were only mildly interested in finding out whether the most innovative ones are in the schools. The following appears to us to be a checklist of reasonable expectations for the schools, given the frequency with which the concepts behind them have been endorsed over the years.

---

**First, classroom practices would be guided by rather clearly discernible educational objectives which, in turn, would reflect larger school-wide and system-wide agreement on school function.**

---

The idea that clarification of objectives must precede evaluation of program is decades old in educational parlance.[11] The advent of programmed and computer-assisted instruction has extended and sharpened it.[12] The move toward large-scale curriculum reform financed by offices of the Federal Government has caused state and local school districts to reiterate their prerogatives with respect to determining the ends of education. Given the rhetoric, it would seem not amiss to anticipate rather clear-cut, specified goals for schooling at all levels of responsibility.

---

**Second, it seems reasonable to assume that classroom instruction, particularly in the early years, would be guided by emphasis on "learning how to learn."**

---

Again, to cite current and recent curriculum reform, the central emphasis has been on structural elements and methods in the subject disciplines, on knowing and the nature of knowing.[13] There is now too much knowledge to "cover" even if this were a desirable approach to learning. To paraphrase Joseph J. Schwab: it is no longer difficult to select and package for instruction those few, most important bits and pieces of knowledge; it is impossible.[14] One might expect to find, then, that "teaching as telling" has now been replaced by many opportunities to explore, to try, to test, to inquire, and to discover for oneself. The so-called new mathematics implies more than updated content. Almost always it also implies "learning by discovery," induction rather than deduction.

---

**Third, one might well expect that the subject matter employed to teach children how to learn would evidence considerable intrinsic appeal for these pupils.**

---

The importance of this idea came to the fore early in this century and was vigorously affirmed by such spokesmen as John Dewey, Alfred North Whitehead, and William H. Kilpatrick. For decades, teachers have been exhorted to select learning opportunities with the needs and interests of their pupils uppermost. Even in the discipline-centered approach to curriculum development of the past fifteen years, learning packages have been planned with an eye to the readiness and potential interests of the learners. One might well expect to find most classrooms today bubbling with the enthusiasm of youngsters involved with salient ideas and absorbing substance.

---

Fourth, and closely related to the preceding expectation, one might assume with confidence that "the golden age of instructional materials" is almost everywhere evident in the schools.

---

Attractive books for children virtually pour from the presses. The 1930's gave birth to educational radio and the 1950's to educational television. The catalogues of several major companies present a rich diet of films and filmstrips for all age and grade levels. For years, educational reformers have been cautioning educators about textbooks, urging use of a wide assortment of instructional materials. Tapes and records not only offer the flexibility to deal with individual differences in children but also offer the convenience of easy use and storage. One might assume that he need only visit any school — the one in your neighborhood or in ours — to see in wide use a magnificent array of instructional materials and devices. Only the computer, because of its relative recency and high cost, might be expected to be conspicuous by its absence.[15]

---

Fifth, one would expect today's schools to pay considerable attention to and make substantial provision for individual differences among students.

---

The nature of these differences, although needing to be still more extensively studied, has been documented sufficiently to reveal some of their relevance for educational practice.[16] Arguments for such recent innovations as nongrading, team teaching, and modular scheduling have been based in large part on data pertaining to individual differences. Similarly, programmed instruction, individually prescribed instruction, and computer-assisted instruction derive some of their salience from differences in learning rates among students. For several years, the topic "individualizing instruction" has ranked at the top in popularity at in-service workshops and institutes for teachers and principals. One might well expect to find extensive provision for individual differences in the way schools are organized, children are grouped in the classroom, books and other instructional materials are distributed and used, instruction and learning proceed, and so on.

Sixth, one might expect today's teachers to make rather substantial use of basic principles of learning and instruction.

There probably is more agreement on the need for educational psychology courses in preparing teachers and on the content of such courses than on any other courses and subject matter in the standard professional sequence for teachers.[17] These principles include motivation, reinforcement, transfer of training, goal setting, evaluating before and after teaching, and so on. Recently, there has been renewed interest in and studies on the importance of warmth, acceptance, and encouragement as factors in enhancing learning. All of these ideas have found fresh expression through special proposals for educating children whose progress in the schools is handicapped by physical, mental, emotional, and environmental limitations or aberrations. Schools and classrooms should be, then, not only pleasant places to spend a thousand hours each year but also living examples of applied pedagogical and learning theory.

---

**Seventh, very closely related to the sixth expectation, one might expect today's classrooms to be laboratories in group dynamics and productive human interaction.**

---

"Group dynamics" became a cult in the late 1940's and early 1950's. But since then, the central ideas have found their way into the teacher education curriculum, particularly in courses on pupil guidance. Thousands of prints of the now classic films on authoritarian, democratic, and laissez-faire leadership styles have been worn out.[18] The concepts of the National Training Laboratories have been woven into the operation of business and industry as well as, presumably, public education. One would expect to find substantial use of group discussion techniques, with youngsters assuming leadership roles and evaluating the productivity of their participation.

---

**Eighth, one would expect to find flexible standards of evaluation, with increasing attention to the actual performance of children, rather than comparison with grade, age, or group norms.**

---

Much has been written about "the tyranny of testing"; teachers have been particularly outspoken in protesting that tests do not tell much and must not be too literally interpreted; and grade standards of performance have been under critical fire for decades. These protests against uniform evaluation standards and procedures are supported by the increasing evidence about and concern for individual differences among students. Many schools now claim to be nongraded[19] and, of course, nongrading and uniform evaluative practices are incompatible; but even where classes are ostensibly graded, one would expect to find concern for individuality applied in determining the quality and adequacy of pupil performance.

---

**Ninth, one would expect to find comparable flexibility in determining both the appropriate settings for learning and the most appropriate persons to participate in instructional activities.**

---

School and classroom are, at best, pitifully inadequate laboratories for life's experiments and lessons, no matter how enriched by bringing in the outside world vicariously through films, television, and other media. Often, the advent of another day should see children scattering to field, pond, museum, library, zoo, or nearby industry. Obviously, this cannot be if our conception of a learning group is 28 children and a teacher. The concept of team teaching, introduced in the mid-1950's and widely disseminated since, proposes virtually any size group and a team of human and inanimate instructional resources.[20] The community is rich with athletes, musicians, artists, linguists, engineers, toy makers, and professional workers who would be delighted to teach for an hour or a day. Some communities maintain extensive inventories of such human and material resources for learning and teaching. One would not expect to find, today, teaching and learning to be largely circumscribed by classroom walls, certified teachers, and a teacher per class group of 28 or so.

---

Tenth, one might reasonably expect to find the traditional reading and listening activities of the primary years considerably expanded and enriched, not only by more vibrant attention to mathematics, but also by considerable attention to the natural and social sciences and, perhaps, to a lesser degree, the arts.[21]

---

One would expect, further, that this enrichment would be carried beyond mere balance and variety in subjects to variety in pedagogical procedure and learning medium. There have been major curricular projects not only in mathematics but also in science and social studies, projects which have extended downward into the primary years. The arts have been neglected, we know, but play, dance, music, and literature generally are regarded as appropriate and important for young children in the primary years as well as in the kindergarten. And, of course, one would expect the entire elementary-school program to be enriched by the plethora of aids to learning presumably available.

Ten is a good round figure with which to stop. We might have set forth other "reasonable expectations" for today's schools but these appear to summarize for us the central thrusts of assumed contemporary progress. None is so recent nor so esoteric as to suggest unfamiliarity and unacceptability to educators.

The matter of "proof" enters here. Educational research provides no one-to-one relationship between findings and school practices. A reasonable expectation for educational research is that it provide, over time, a body of lore which, if drawn upon, would steadily raise the level of intelligence in educational decisions. The preceding ideas appear to stem from such lore but, clearly, they stand to be replaced by subsequent inquiry — and by certain of tomorrow's fashions.

## Notes

1. Moshe and Sarah Smilansky, "Bases for Intellectual Advancement of Culturally Disadvantaged Children." ed. John I. Goodlad, *Human Behavior and Childhood Schooling* (Worthington, Ohio: Charles A. Jones Publishing Co., in press).

2. Jerome S. Bruner, *The Process of Education* (Cambridge, Mass.: Harvard University Press, 1960), p. 55.

3. James B. Conant, *The Education of American Teachers* (New York: McGraw-Hill Book Co., 1963); John I. Goodlad, *School Curriculum Reform in the United States* (New York: The Fund for the Advancement of Education, 1964); John I. Goodlad with Renata von Stoephasius and M. Frances Klein, *The Changing School Curriculum* (New York: The Fund for the Advancement of Education, 1966).

4. Martin Mayer, *The Schools* (New York: Harper & Bros., 1961), p. 426.

5. Paul Goodman, *Compulsory Mis-Education* (New York: Horizon Press, 1964), p. 10.

6. Bel Kaufman, *Up the Down Staircase* (Englewood Cliffs, N. J.: Prentice-Hall, Inc., 1964); Jane Bergen et al., *Robots in the Classroom* (New York: Exposition Press, 1955); Nat Hentoff, *Our Children Are Dying* (New York: The Viking Press, 1966).

7. The many requests for consulting services to the staff of the University Elementary School contributed, in some degree, to the decision to

create the League of Cooperating Schools. We saw the possibility of working directly with a group of very different schools in Southern California in order to implement the ideas guiding the University Elementary School. The League project, from 1966 to 1971, provided a unique laboratory for studying the problems which school faculties encounter when they seek to implement many of the changes which have been recommended for the schools. For further elaboration, see John I. Goodlad, "The League of Cooperating Schools," *The California Journal of Instructional Improvement,* vol. IX, December, 1966, pp. 213-218.

8. John I. Goodlad, *Some Propositions in Search of Schools* (Washington, D.C.: Department of Elementary School Principals, 1962).

9. The idea of schools teaching a rhetoric of conclusions rather than how to inquire is effectively developed in Joseph J. Schwab, "Education and the Structure of the Disciplines." (Paper prepared for the Project on the Instructional Program of the Public Schools, National Education Association. Washington, D.C., September, 1961).

10. One of many steps toward emphasizing the temporary, dispensable character of the school is to pay less attention to school as a place. It is encouraging to note that some schools are beginning to pay less attention to the need for children to enter each day a place called "school" and to emphasize more the learning resources all around us which lie ready to be exploited through appropriate processes of inquiry.

11. Robert Armstrong, Terry Cornell, Robert Kraner, E. Wayne Roberson, *Development and Evaluation of Behavioral Objectives* (Worthington, Ohio: Charles A. Jones Publishing Co., 1970).

12. Interest in behavioral statements of objectives was sharply stimulated by Robert F. Mager, *Preparing Objectives for Programed Instruction* (San Francisco: Fearon Publishers, 1962). More recently, the refinement of educational objectives and the planning of instruction for their attainment have been further clarified in three little volumes by W. James Popham and Eva L. Baker, *Establishing Instructional Goals, Planning an Instructional Sequence,* and *Systematic Instruction* (New York: Prentice-Hall, Inc., 1970).

13. Jack R. Frymier and Horace C. Hawn, *Curriculum Improvement for Better Schools* (Worthington, Ohio: Charles A. Jones Publishing Co. 1970).

14. Joseph J. Schwab, "Education and the Structure of the Disci-

plines." (Paper prepared for the Project on the Instructional Program of the Public Schools, National Education Association, Washington, D.C., September 1961.)

15. The decade of the '60's ended and the decade of the '70's began with the computer still used primarily for experimental work in instruction. Wide-scale use for instructional purposes still lies in the future. See John I. Goodlad, John F. O'Toole, Jr., and Louise L. Tyler, *Computers and Information Systems in Education* (New York: Harcourt, Brace & World, Inc., 1966); and John W. Loughary and Associates, *Man-Machine Systems in Education* (New York: Harper & Row, 1966).

16. For analyses of individual differences and school practices designed to cope with them, see National Society for the Study of Education, *Individualizing Instruction.* LXI *Yearbook,* Part I (Chicago: University of Chicago Press, 1962); Virgil M. Howes, Madeline C. Hunter, Robert E. Keuscher, and Louise L. Tyler, *Individualization of Instruction: A Search* (Los Angeles, Calif.: Educational Inquiry, Incorporated, 1967). Now available through The Bookstore, University of California, Los Angeles.

17. See, for example, James B. Conant, *The Education of American Teachers* (New York: McGraw-Hill Book Co., 1963).

18. The work depicted in the films is reported in Ralph K. White and Ronald D. Lippitt, *Autocracy and Democracy; an Experimental Inquiry* (New York: Harper & Brothers, 1960).

19. For an excellent bibliography on nongrading which includes selected doctoral dissertations, see Henry J. Otto and Associates, *Nongradedness: An Elementary School Evaluation* (Austin: The University of Texas, 1969), pp. 4-9. Also, see Lillian K. Spitzer, "School Organization and Facilities," in *Selected Readings for the Elementary School Administrator.* Part V, |I|D|E|A| Bibliography Series (Melbourne, Fla.: |I|D|E|A| Informational Services Division, 1969).

20. For more information on team teaching, consult the bibliography prepared by Lillian K. Spitzer, "Selected Readings on Team Teaching" (Melbourne, Fla.: |I|D|E|A|, Information and Services Division, 1969).

21. During the '60's in particular, the National Science Foundation provided financial resources to update and increase the teaching of natural sciences in the schools. Other foundations and the Federal Gov-

ernment have supported the social sciences and, to a lesser degree, the arts. For a report of the curriculum reform movement characterizing the late '50's and early '60's, see John I. Goodlad with Renata von Stoephasius and M. Frances Klein, *The Changing School Curriculum* (New York: The Fund for the Advancement of Education, 1966).

# Chapter Two

# Categories for Observing and Evaluating Childhood Schooling

Our preliminary decision to look deeply into current practices in the first four years of school was clinched by a summer experience of several in our group. Increasingly, we had found ourselves to be critical of the intent and the practice of "preparing children for school." First, we believe that no period in life should be sacrificed to any other; good education today is the best preparation for tomorrow. Second, we had doubts then and have more serious doubts now about the value and quality of what preschool children are to be prepared *for*. We decided to bring together in the summer a group of children comprising those for whom preschool education was especially intended and those already in the schools these preschoolers were destined to attend. We set out to recruit for summer session approximately 70 children between the ages of four and eight — black, brown, and white children from a central section of the city. Contrary to anticipated community disinterest (we had been told that recruitment would be difficult), restricting enrollment became a serious public relations problem. We were still turning parents and children away on the opening day and ended up with more children than we had planned for initially.

We had been informed, also, that these children would be, for the most part, passive and unresponsive in school, to the point of disinterest and nonlearning. Finally, we had been advised to provide a more "controlling," regimented program than the one we conduct for our enrollees during the regular school year.

Our actual experience that summer ran quite counter to advice and admonitions. The children were, indeed, nonplussed over the indoor-outdoor environment of trees, dirt, sand, boulders, and ravine, an environment replete with blocks, books, toys, tools, wheeled vehicles, and even ducks and bantams. Initially overwhelmed, they kept asking when school was going to begin! Soon, however, they entered vigorously into the possibilities of this environment, moving quickly from stimulus to stimulus before settling primarily on a few. Interestingly, girls soon became preoccupied with "feminine" activities: cooking, sewing, and playing house. Boys concentrated on running, cycling, sliding, and constructing — and, more than the victims appreciated, chasing the ducks.

Teachers, too, were busy: intervening when brawls became too heated, rescuing our animals from too vigorous embraces, seeking child-interpreters for requests spoken in Spanish, learning children's names, habits, and interests. Little by little, they began to move into situations offering opportunities to push childhood curiosity a little further, to use small group activities for the stimulation of conversation, and to show that picture or story books offered another view of daily experiences.

Where do these ideas come from? Again, this category overlaps with others and the overlap is deliberate. We believe it is good to come at significant concepts from several different vantage points.

7. *Inquiry.* Two indices are of primary interest here. First, is the process of learning one of seeking out or being given conclusions? (Category 2, again.) Second, what kinds of closure appear to be sought — closure on facts, ways of applying knowledge, or possible hypotheses about phenomena?

8. *Independence.* What we have in mind here is the framework of control and freedom guiding the way children conduct themselves in the environment. Is each possible line of activity governed by a rule? By the teacher monitoring each act *ad hoc,* so to speak? By some agreed-upon set of expectations? Do children move quietly about the room attending to their needs? Do they ask permission to leave their seats, for example? Do they sit at their desks for fixed periods of time?

9. *Curriculum Balance.* The interest in this category is with the range of organized human experience with which the class seems to deal. Are subject matter and activities concentrated in a few fields or spread across the major divisions of knowledge? Are emphases identifiable?

10. *Curricular Adaptation.* The curriculum comes into the classroom through textbooks, curriculum guides and bulletins, "packages" of materials, the teacher's accumulated experience, or all of these. The question here has to do with the modifications and adaptations, if any, that take place in the light of immediate realities. Do the children get involved in how they are going to use and adapt what is offered for their education? Does the teacher modify the curriculum in the light of her knowledge of the class group?

11. *Ceilings and Floors of Expectancy.* What kinds of pupil performance and attainment levels are reflected in the classroom activities and processes? Do single-grade standards

seem to prevail or is the spread between ceilings and floors increased to encompass the range of individual differences? Here we get at the predominance of concepts relevant to graded or nongraded programs.

12. *Staff Utilization.* Does each teacher appear to be working independent of colleagues? This has been the traditional elementary-school pattern. We need to find out here whether classes remain intact all day with one teacher, whether other teachers come in for special purposes, whether teachers sometimes share planning and teaching, and whether instructional groups sometimes are made up of students from several classes. We run into such terminology as the self-contained classroom, departmentalization, and team teaching as ways of describing the organization of curriculum, children, and teachers.

This list pays little attention to the relatively subtle aspects of instruction: goal setting, use of learning theory, and application of pedagogical principles derived from the behavioral sciences. While these appear to us to be enormously important, trials with our preliminary check sheet had discouraged us from proceeding further with any rigorous attempt to document their classroom use.


## School and Classroom Observation

With discussion of such categories and indices behind us, a small group returned once again to the matter of providing a reasonably simple guide to the collection of anecdotal and interview data. (See Appendix.) Also, all of those who were to visit in schools entered into sessions designed to develop some competence in conducting interviews, under direction of the school's social worker. And a new round of trial observations began, this time for the purpose of improving inclusiveness in the anecdotal records and checking agreement among the three individuals selected to interpret them.

Meanwhile, letters were sent out to request permission to visit and to explain the purpose of our coming. One large city system denied permission; later, a second denied permission to interview teachers and principals. In the initial round, our teachers observed in 158 classrooms of 67 schools in 26 school districts. These were almost entirely in or around the major cities of 13 states and included a nationwide geographic spread. Findings and generalizations are based on 150 of these 158 classrooms.

Initial visits were followed by observations in 27 classrooms of 12 schools located in or near seven cities of four southwestern states. These schools enrolled primarily Mexican-American children, with the exception of one with predominantly black boys and girls. Data from these observations were not included in the summaries but served instead to confirm generalizations and to support certain tentative conclusions about the education of minority group children presumed to be environmentally disadvantaged. Finally, several members of the staff joined with a new group of observers in visiting 75 classrooms in 31 school districts of California, classrooms chosen at random from schools identified as having reputations for innovating. The data are not included in the summaries but proved useful for checking generalizations and conclusions about the conduct of elementary schooling.

Our findings presented here are based on 150 of the initial group of 158 classroom visits. But our strongest generalizations and conclusions carry the added weight of being supported by visits to a total of 260 classrooms.

The staff made every possible effort to get into three groups of schools: schools considered by administration (usually represented by a ranking member of the superintendent's supporting group of professionals) to be average, run of the mill, with respect to resources and programs; schools supposedly conducting some special or innovative activities; and schools enrolling a large proportion of environmentally disadvantaged children. We attempted to maintain these distinctions for purposes of data analysis but found them to have limited usefulness. A few interesting differences among the groups appeared but, in general, the configurations of data from one approximated those from the other two. These differences and similiarities are discussed in Chapter Three.

Observers gathered data from three sources: interviews with teachers, interviews with principals, and observation of classroom activities. The first of these proved vexing, far beyond what had been anticipated. Elementary-school teachers are on the run all day. Interviewing them is somewhat akin to interviewing jockeys during a horse race. And the average elementary school is an eggcrate with corridors, each compartment of the crate occupied by a teacher and 28 children. There is neither the place, then, nor the opportunity to sit in quiet conversation with elementary-school teachers. Interviews with principals presented few problems. Our staff visited three classrooms each day, preparing anecdotal records of visits which were, with three exceptions, more than 45 minutes long. All three sources of data were then used in writing the summaries of observations.

After raw data had been obtained and written up by our observers, three members of the staff analyzed them. Independent judgments of the same record, subsequent checks, and then discussion among all three soon produced a high level of interpretative agreement and a common vocabulary.

We have implied some major limitations of the study. Others should be made explicit. In spite of basic agreement on educational values and training sessions on observing and recording, it soon became apparent that our staff members varied in their interviewing and writing skills. Anecdotal records varied in their comprehensiveness and in the degree to which observational data were separated from evaluations without data.

Then, although we emphasized our desire to observe "typical" activities and to be as unobtrusive as the desks, there is little doubt that some teachers performed for our staff. Perhaps all did, in some fashion and to some degree. No doubt our findings are contaminated throughout by this tendency. It seems reasonable to assume that the teachers slightly excelled their usual performances in the direction of their own perceptions of good teaching or of what they surmised ours to be.

In spite of the good intentions of our staff to gather comparable data, circumstances often prevented our doing so. Sometimes interviews with teachers were conducted under most unfavorable circumstances. Sometimes, lessons were characterized by such a limited range of activities over so long a period that one simply had to give up the attempt to be comprehensive within the framework of our guide to classroom observation.

The sample of classrooms, particularly when divided into grade levels, is small and concentrated on the city and its periphery. But metropolitan concerns, especially educational ones, increasingly predominate in domestic affairs. The size of the sample is offset somewhat by the depth of treatment and the consistency of findings.

Our travellers collected an enormous amount of material, material which provided not only amazing consistency in the quantifiable data but also repetitive impressionistic agreement to the point of analyst boredom. It is this high level of agreement among observers, observers who are themselves teachers, that gives our account of what goes on behind school and classroom doors whatever viability it may possess.

# Notes

1. The story of these children and the experiences we had with them that summer are recorded in a film, "The Summer Children," available from Academic Communications Facility, the University of California, Los Angeles. The production of this film was made possible by a grant from the Fund for the Advancement of Education of the Ford Foundation.

2. Among the many studies examined, the following provided some useful ideas in our efforts to refine strategies: Marie M. Hughes, *et al.*, *Assessment of the Quality of Teaching in Elementary Schools* (Salt Lake City: University of Utah, 1959); Ned A. Flanders, *Teacher Influence, Pupil Attitudes and Achievement* (Cooperative Research Project no. 397, U.S. Office of Education. Minneapolis, Minn.: University of Minnesota Press, 1960); Ned A. Flanders, *Teacher Influence, Pupil Attitudes and Achievement* (OE-25040, Cooperative Research Monograph no. 12. Washington, D.C.: U.S. Government Printing Office, 1965); Arno A. Bellack, "The Language of the Classroom: Meanings Communicated in High School Teaching," *Theories of Instruction*, ed. James B. Macdonald and Robert R. Leeper (Washington, D.C.: Association for Supervision and Curriculum Development, 1965); B. Othanel Smith, "Toward a Theory of Teaching," *Theory and Research in Teaching*, ed. Arno A. Bellack (New York: Teachers College Press, 1963).

# Chapter Three

# Observation Findings in Schools and Classrooms

Magazines of national scope, the daily press, and many books have proclaimed a revolution in our schools. To what extent has this widely-heralded revolution been a reality? It seemed to us that our look at schools and classrooms would provide a basis for answering such a question. Our findings are better suited to narrative than to tabular, quantitative presentation; the latter form too often implies certainty, regardless of whatever cautions the researcher sets forth.

The summary describing schools and resources is based on 158 classrooms in 67 schools. The summary based on observations and interviews pertains to 150 of these classrooms: 32 kindergartens, 45 first-grade, 26 second-grade, and 18 third-grade classes; and 29 classes at these grade levels classified as "special." The numbers of classes classified as enrolling a large proportion of disadvantaged children were 20, 26, 15, 7, and 13 respectively. Of the 150 classrooms, then, 81 enrolled a large proportion of disadvantaged children; 69 were classified as regular in that they did not contain a disproportionate number of such children.

## Schools and Resources

Enrollment in the schools visited ranged from 130 to 1,850, with an average of 669 pupils per school and 28 per classroom. The average number of teachers was 24, with a range of 4 to 65. Many of the schools in our sample enjoyed the services of specialists, although in all but the largest these persons were shared with other schools in the district. Music specialists constituted the largest group, with more than half of the schools (38) having access to such personnel, most of whom were itinerant. About half (33) were served by specialists in the personnel field: psychologists, social workers, or guidance counselors. Physical education specialists (31) also constituted a comparatively large group. About a third of our schools had access to librarians (23); medical, dental, or *para*-medical services (21); speech pathologists (20); and specialists in remedial reading (19). Sixteen schools used art specialists and 10 used specialists in foreign languages, usually through their programs for bilingual students. A few schools employed or used, part time, specialists in mathematics, science, and the social studies but the total of these was low (10). Five used teacher aides and 2 made use of teacher training specialists.

We do not know how much our findings in this area might have been slanted by the urban bias of the sample. Certainly, the buildings visited were more characteristic of older, urban schools than of fast-growing suburban districts. School plants ranged in age from 1 to 79 years, with an average of 25. Only one in three was of the single-floor variety; the rest were two stories or more.

Most of the schools were graded and followed the modified, self-contained pattern of classroom organization; that is, one teacher assumed responsibility for the class most of the time, but occasionally was relieved or assisted by a special resource person. Ten schools claimed to be nongraded, at least in part, and 12 claimed to be using some form of team teaching. We shall have more to say later about these reported organizational modifications.

About half of our schools were involved as single schools or as part of their districts in projects or activities supported by supplementary funds from local, state, federal, or private sources. Head Start and projects under the Elementary and Secondary Education Act (Title III) predominated. Almost all of the local funds were sharply restricted to such items as bus services, libraries, and routine equipment or supplies.

The curriculum framework for most of the schools in our sample was supplied, so far as we were able to determine, by guides prepared at local, county, or state level. These and textbooks provided the major sources of the schools' curricula, a finding which is in agreement with other surveys.[1] The books of three companies—Ginn; Scott, Foresman; and Macmillan —predominated in the reading field. Materials for mathematics were distributed over a half-dozen companies, with some of the newer, experimental projects represented.

Two-thirds of our schools used one of three, well-known, standardized tests—Metropolitan, Iowa, or Otis—in testing the achievement of their pupils, with the Metropolitan accounting for as many schools as the other two tests combined. We were surprised at the range of tests actually being used in the schools during the year we visited, some 26 different ones being employed to appraise achievement, aptitude, reading readiness, and special abilities or psychological factors, although these last were rarely tested in any formal way. It is clear that the schools in our sample stayed almost exclusively with measurement of the traditional areas, achievement and intelligence, and measured them with the well-known, long-established instruments.

In regard to reporting to parents, half of our sample combined report cards with some kind of conference with parents. About a fifth used report cards exclusively; and only two schools employed the conference procedure exclusively. This is one area in which our information was far from complete.

Once inside the schools, we were interested, of course, in knowing something about the structure of the classrooms, the pupils enrolled, and the teachers. The modified, self-contained, graded pattern stood out clearly, with about 80 percent (122 classrooms) using it. The remainder reported some attempt at nongrading or team teaching but we found that many of these used the "reading levels" approach to homogeneous grouping in the case of the former and departmentalization in the case of the latter, and did not, therefore, approximate the flexibility normally associated with these two organizational structures.

Slightly more than half of the classrooms visited enrolled children from urban settings and a large proportion of these could be classified as being environmentally or culturally disadvantaged. We maintained a separation of data for classes classified as enrolling predominantly urban, disadvantaged children.

Some of our teachers were beginners; one had taught for 40 years. The average amount of experience was 12 years, and the average time spent in the grade currently taught was 7.5 years. They devoted, on the average, nine hours each week, outside of classroom teaching, to paper work and another three to matters of school administration. Most saw themselves as having considerable flexibility with respect to adapting the curriculum.

Clearly, succeeding summaries of classroom practices are not based on a sample of largely innovative schools, schools which are departing from standard practices and setting the pace in breaking with tradition, so far as their general image is concerned. From the observations of our visiting staff and from analyzing their reports, one gets an impression of conventional, middle-aged buildings; experienced, dedicated, and rather hard-working teachers; conventional, self-contained classrooms, enjoying intermittent access to specialized resources; the usual array of textbooks; and both reporting and testing procedures which have characterized schools for some years. Within this broad and rather uniform picture are a few splashes of contrast representing movement toward some of the innovations which have been predominant in educational parlance for a decade.

## Classroom Practices

For convenience and simplicity, we decided to report the findings from classroom observation in categories approximating those which our observers used in collecting the data. We return in the succeeding section, however, to broad categories encompassing our list of reasonable expectations and our initial discussions of what we had hoped to learn from the visits (see Chapter One and Chapter Two). These permit us to combine more readily all of the evidence from which concluding generalizations and observations are drawn. For ease of comprehension, we have combined for each category both the description and summary of data for it.

### 1. Instructional Process and Learning Climate

#### 1.1 Instructional Event

Instructional event means simply the activity under way at the time of visitation: reading, listening to stories, counting, drawing, etc. Sometimes, several such activities were under way simultaneously.

The activity observed most frequently and consistently at all grade levels, with the exception of kindergarten, was reading. When one adds to this the scattering of related activities—instruction in phonics, writing, spelling, listening to stories, discussing library books, studying the elements of language—it becomes clear that the language arts, in one form or another, dominated formal instruction in our sample of classrooms. One significant difference between classes enrolling a predominance of disadvantaged children and so-called regular classes was a much greater incidence of reading among the former at the first-grade level, followed by a rapid decline in grades two and three. Whereas reading dominated in the disadvantaged first-grade classes by a two-to-one ratio over the regular classes, second-grade differences were negligible, and the ratio changed to about four-to-one dominance in the regular classes by the third grade.

The second most frequently observed event was what we termed "independent activities." These were activities selected by the children from a range of possibilities, with relatively little teacher direction and subsequent supervision. Whereas in kindergarten, and to a lesser degree in the first grade, these independent activities involved physical movement (particularly manipulation of blocks, puzzles, toys, etc.), they shifted by the third grade to a narrower range of "academic" work: filling in workbooks, reading, looking up words in the dictionary, and so on. Independence in selection and subsequent performance showed a much stronger teacher hand. Kindergarten activity almost denied classification; third-grade activity easily lent itself to a few, subject-oriented categories. The sheer quantity of independent activities observed fell off markedly after the first grade.

Interestingly, a clear difference between regular and disadvantaged classes appeared. The kind of free, self-chosen activity described here was scarcely discernible in the disadvantaged classes during our visits but was apparently a teacher-determined program frequently referred to as "activity time." Usually, this constituted a sharp break from the more academic side of the kindergarten program; singing, games, and rhythms (moving to music) predominated. Our visitors to first-grade classes viewed very little of this sort of thing among the disadvantaged classes but a great deal of the independent activities described in the preceding paragraph. Both groups of activities fell off sharply thereafter and were not observed by our group in any third-grade classes in the disadvantaged group.

Arithmetic, singing and music, and physical education were relatively high-frequency categories, with the last two dropping off more sharply in grades two and three for disadvantaged classes. Arithmetic tended to hold up most consistently among these groups of activities for all classes and grade levels. The traditional "show and tell" showed up from time to time in kindergarten and the first two grades.

All of the preceding categories together account for over 85 percent of the classroom events observed. Social studies and science trailed far behind, with the former observed only once in disadvantaged classes (at the third grade level). Virtually all of the rest of the activities might be classified as classroom routine: changing from one activity to the next, cleaning up after the previous activity, dismissal, snack time, opening exercises, and in the kindergarten, resting or chatting together.

A word about what we did not observe is in order. Although there has been much talk about the value of dramatic play and dramatization for young children, we observed very little of either (one instance of the former and three of the latter); similarly, with perceptual motor activities, designed to develop coordination of brain, eye, and limbs, and with training in listening. We observed audio-visual equipment in some classrooms (more about this in the section on materials and equipment) but rarely saw tape recorders and movie projectors in use.

General conclusions cannot be drawn from one category of data; and yet no category can be ignored, since the cumulative picture depends on all of them. Data were derived from snapshots taken during a visitation period of 45 minutes or longer—only three visits were for a shorter period. Of course, we must assume some distortion or departure from regular practice because of the presence of visitors.

### 1.2 Teacher Involvement

An area of great interest to us was the teacher's involvement in or orientation to her task. This category is subtle and subject more than most to impressionistic interpretation. We judged the teacher's involvement to be "low" when the record contained such comments as: teacher seemed almost bored; instruction routine, uninspired, unchallenging; teacher seemed to have put little thought or imagination into planning, teacher showed no interest or enthusiasm. We judged teacher involvement to be "high" on the basis of such comments as these: teacher obviously enjoys what she is doing; teacher responsive to children; teacher tries different approaches on the basis of pupil reaction; the children show interest in the content or the activity; teacher has planned carefully and thoughtfully, is seeking to relate to children; teacher is enthusiastic and spontaneous. In between were comments which seemed to indicate a well organized but not exciting role on the part of the teacher: teacher busy but instruction is cut and dried; orderly with few distractions; well organized but routine; the children have work to do and tend to keep at it. Descriptions like this resulted in an "average" rating for teacher involvement.

As is to be expected with phenomena of this kind and such subjective classifications for dealing with them, the "average" rating predominated. The teachers showed evidence of having planned for their work and proceeded to effect their plans in a reasonably organized fashion, with a minimum of distraction or spontaneity. About one in seven was rated as having high involvement; about two in seven as having low involvement. There were no marked differences between teachers in regular and in disadvantaged classes. When grade levels were compared, both kindergarten and first-grade teachers showed up somewhat disproportionately on the high side of the involvement scale and only about one kindergarten teacher in six was rated as low.

One item from the data would be worth following up with a larger sample. For our own interest, we kept a separate tally of classes which were organized for some special purpose: remedial reading, instruction in English as a second language, and so on. These we further subdivided into "regular" and disadvantaged." The regular group had an almost bimodal distribution with respect to teacher involvement, the distribution in the low category being the greater (almost half the small sample of teachers in the group). No such distribution showed up for the equally small group of disadvantaged classes in this "special" category; their teachers were largely in the average designation. It would be interesting to see whether teachers in such classes nationwide distribute themselves in like fashion, the extent to which teachers self-select or are assigned to such classes, and why they so select when given the opportunity to do so.

### 1.3 Teacher Attitudes

We were interested here in finding out something about the way teachers related themselves to children. Again, we used three categories to suggest positive and negative as opposites and a kind of neutrality between these two. A positive rating emerged from such terms on the observational record as accepting, approving, concerned, empathetic, encouraging, fair, gentle, kind, helpful, supportive, warm, and so on. A negative rating resulted from such terms as aloof, angry, bored, brusque, cold, derogatory, disapproving, disrespectful, harsh, impatient, and insensitive. Middle-ground terms included businesslike, commanding, demanding, condescending, distant, dominant, formal, impersonal, and perfunctory. This category suffers perhaps even more from intuitive and impressionistic reactions and from having both to put reactions into words and to place a further evaluative judgment upon them. What we have here, then, is a kind of semantic differentiating which rather than being the teachers' own felt reaction to children is observers' reactions to those observed.

The teachers in our sample came through strongly positive on the matter of attitudes toward children. The words most commonly used, far surpassing any others, to describe this attitude were supportive and warm. These two words together accounted for over 20 percent of all the words used which we considered reflective of teacher attitudes toward children and for over 40 percent of the words we judged to be positive in tone. Other words of positive connotation, trailing far behind the first two in frequency, were relaxed, positive, interested, friendly, and accepting. No single word of negative connotation captured as much as 20 percent of all negative, attitudinal words nor as much as 2 percent of the total of attitudinal words. Inconsistent and cold appeared most frequently. Formal, directive, and demanding accounted for about 12 percent of all words considered reflective of teacher attitudes toward children. These three words were followed in frequency by authoritarian, businesslike, distant, and controlling. These words, although not conveying much about the strength of attitudes toward children, add considerably to our picture of the total classroom learning climate.

Positive attitudinal descriptive words by our observers exceeded the total of neutral and negative words (by a ratio of about five to four). Strongly negative words accounted for less than 12 percent of the total. When we scrutinized the data more carefully, some interesting findings fell out. Kindergarten and first-grade teachers garnered more than their "share" of positive comments. Positive words exceeded the total of neutral and negative words by a ratio of about three to two for first-grade teachers and nearly two to one for kindergarten teachers. But, interestingly, both also exceeded the teacher sample as a whole in percentage of negative words, the kindergarten teachers going up to almost 20 percent in this category and the first-grade group to nearly 17 percent.

The second-grade group was the only one with an excess of neutral and negative descriptions over positive ones, by a ratio of nearly two to one. It also was the only grade with an excess of neutral over positive statements. The percentage of negative words was identical with that of the first-grade group. The ratio of positive to neutral and negative combined for the third grade was about five to four, or comparable with the total sample, but negative statements accounted for only 7 percent of the third-grade total.

A further breakdown of the data into our very tentative regular and disadvantaged classes revealed an almost identical distribution. Also, our small, special group of classrooms broke down as for the total, no bimodal situation this time appearing.

## 1.4 Children's Involvement

We were interested in children's involvement in their learning tasks in much the same way we were interested in teachers' involvement in teaching tasks. We judged this involvement to be low when our observers reported that "only three children participated in a total class discussion lesson during a period of 30 minutes"; or that most of the children seemed not to understand what was going on; or that the children responded only briefly or not at all to teacher queries. We judged as high involvement comments that the children participated with vigor and enthusiasm; the children were busy and independent, not easily distracted; and the children turned readily to new tasks on completing the present one. We concluded average involvement when the record told us that the children were doing about what was asked and expected, no more no less; they were busy, quiet, and orderly but evidenced little or no enthusiasm and spontaneity; or they were not inclined to seek out new tasks on their own.

The overall picture here was similar in general contour to that of the teachers; but analysis reveals greater variability. In about one class in five, the children were judged to have high involvement, in contrast to a one-in-seven rating in this category for the teachers. The two groups were almost identical for low involvement, with about 25 percent in this category. Thus, the greater movement away from center for the children was caused by greater incidence of high involvement. About three classes in five showed average pupil involvement, in contrast to about two classes in three for teacher involvement.

Kindergarten and first-grade classes showed up somewhat disproportionately on the high side of the involvement scale, thus following the pattern for teachers. Unlike the teacher pattern, however, these classes with high involvement of children were disproportionately in the disadvantaged group. Whereas only 2 of 20 such classes had revealed teacher involvement to be high, 8 were reported to have high children's involvement. The patterns for children and teachers in so-called regular classes were almost identical. The slightly bimodal distribution for teachers in our small group of special classes did not appear. Again, however, the classes in the low children's involvement column from this special group were predominantly regular rather than disadvantaged, as had been the case with teachers.

One of the clearest sets of findings from this study stands out particularly sharply when the graph for children's involvement by grades is placed side by side with the graph for teachers' involvement: both fall off sharply after kindergarten and first grade. The frequency of high involvement for grades two and three is low; the frequency of average to low involvement is disproportionately high for both children and teachers. The greater frequency of high involvement for children is accounted for almost entirely by kindergarten and grade one. In our total sample of classes, the second grade stands out as the low point for both children's and teachers' involvement in the ongoing instructional program.

### 1.5 Social-Instructional Interaction

Another important category in our effort to compile a picture of the learning climate had to do with the direction of social interaction during the period of instruction observed. If the teacher directed most of the questions to the children and the children simply responded to the teacher's questions and directions, the interaction pattern was described as teacher to child. Child-to-teacher interaction was judged to occur if the child took the initiative to request help or in some way sought a response from the teacher before the teacher sought a response from him. When the children carried the discussion or lesson among themselves, using or not using the teacher as a resource, we described the process as child-to-child interaction.

Our earlier exposure to the highly scientific techniques for this kind of observation developed by Flanders had alerted us to the hazards and difficulties.[2] These were compounded by the fact that all of these interaction patterns might readily occur during a single observation period. It turned out, however, that single patterns of interaction tended to dominate in most classrooms.

At all grade levels, the teacher-to-child pattern of interaction overwhelmingly prevailed. This was one of the most monotonously recurring pieces of data. The teachers asked questions and the children responded, usually in a few words and phrases and usually correctly — that is, with the response approved or acknowledged as correct by the teacher. It is fair to say that teacher-to-child interaction was the mode in all but about 5 percent of the classes.

This is not to say, however, that the other two patterns did not also occur in most classrooms; with a few exceptions, they simply constituted occasional departures from the norm. Children from time to time sidestepped teacher queries in order to pose questions or observations of their own, and from time to time, attempted or succeeded in some temporary redirection of the lesson. For the most part, however, teacher outflow and command of the situation were such as to make it very difficult for children to enter in any oblique way or to begin goal-directed discussion among themselves. When children did interact with each other, this was usually outside the regular process of instruction and represented a few moments of distraction or respite. It appeared to be a matter of individual teacher tolerance as to the length of time such diversions were permitted to continue. In other words, whatever the pattern in the record — teacher to child, child to teacher, or child to child — it almost invariably was teacher dominated. And the pattern was consistent for all grade levels.

## 1.6 Domain and Level of Instruction

For several years, we have been significantly preoccupied with determination of institutional and instructional objectives, refinement of them, and their use in teaching and evaluation. In processes of staff study and research[3] we have relied heavily on the taxonomical work of Bloom, Krathwohl, and their associates.[4] For this study, we choose to stay away from observations concerning the affective domain because of our limited experience with it. We sought, then, to distinguish between ongoing classroom activities calling primarily for psychomotor involvement and those emphasizing the cognitive. Then, in regard to the latter, we endeavored to distinguish between mere recall of information and various higher levels of understanding, use, and insight.

We found substantial evidence of psychomotor involvement — activities calling for manipulation of objects, the use of large and small muscles, eye-hand coordination — at the kindergarten level, particularly in classes heavily disadvantaged in their enrollment. In fact, they were slightly in excess of the more narrowly cognitive kind of activity. As might be expected, the next highest frequency of psychomotor activity was in the first grade. But the cognitive dominated in the first grade, as it did in the second and third. Further, the cognitive involvement called for was overwhelmingly the recognition or recall of factual material.

Even at kindergarten and first-grade levels, most of the instruction emphasized the ability to remember, to recognize from previous exposure, and to repeat. The symbol for mastery was the accuracy of verbal responses — usually, as stated before, responses to teacher questions. When higher intellectual processes were sought or elicited, they usually involved some display of reading or mathematical comprehension. There was little exploring, hunching, guessing, supposing, at any grade level. The teacher-to-child pattern of interaction apparently was not conducive to this sort of inquiry.

## 1.7 Grouping and Individualizing in Instruction

First, we were interested in finding out about interclass grouping; that is, patterns of combining pupils from two or more grades and classes for instructional purposes. Second, we wanted to find out about teacher practices in intraclass grouping; that is, whether the children in any given classroom were grouped for reading, spelling, or other activities and purposes. Finally, we sought for evidences of individualizing instruction, whatever the grouping pattern. Here, we used a rather strict criterion: whether or not the teacher appeared to have some prior awareness of the individual needs or interests of children and was deliberately providing for them. Admittedly, there is shadowy ground here. For example, in most discussions, teachers at least accept and often encourage a variety of responses from children and this might be regarded as individualizing instruction. But, in such situations, we sought to determine whether this was just a random part of the process of moving a group to "right" answers or whether recognition, encouragement, or guidance of diversity was involved. We were not prepared to include the former in our tally of individualizing instruction.

With the exception of the small cluster of special classes, the classrooms in our sample were overwhelmingly self-contained and had little or no instructional association with each other. The dominant pattern throughout was one grade and one teacher for each class. Many classes, of course, provided in the schedule for some part-time teaching by an itinerant specialist. About one teacher in six reported some kind of cooperative endeavor with one or more other teachers but such evidence of this as we discovered pointed to exchange of children for a subject, particularly for reading in the first grade. Several teachers reported team teaching but we observed only one genuine instance of it in action, involving 3 teachers and 87 children in the second grade.

In our sample of special classes, by contrast, some form of interclass grouping predominated — organizationally, this was the major characteristic of their being special. Twenty-one of 29 classes interchanged children and/or teachers in various ways — almost as many as in the other 131 classrooms making up the total of 150. It would appear that moving children or teachers about in some interclass pattern of grouping is a device considered more frequently when some sort of "special" learning problem or need has been identified in the school or school system.

As is to be expected, there was high incidence of grouping within our sample of first-, second-, and third-grade classes. With very few exceptions, first-grade classes were grouped for reading, usually employing from two to four groups. The second-grade classes had an even higher incidence than the first-grade classes, with grouping extended from reading into other subjects. This expansion into a few other subjects was evident also in our sample of third-grade classes. The frequency of this intraclass grouping fell off in the special classes, presumably because the children in them already were "grouped." There was little difference between regular and disadvantaged classes except in the first grade where the instance was substantially greater for the latter. Since reading and grouping in grade one seem to go together and since first-grade activities in our disadvantaged classes emphasized reading and language activities, this finding and the earlier one appear to be consistent.

With respect to grouping, the kindergarten sample deviated from the rest. Interclass grouping was virtually non-existent and intraclass grouping occurred less often than in any of the subsequent three grades. More than half of the intraclass grouping which we did observe in the kindergarten tended to be rather flexible, according to interest rather than ability or achievement, and organized around an assortment of activities proceeding simultaneously. In the higher grades, however, the groups were "set," organized around achievement, and confined to one subject at a time.

An essential part of our definition of individualization of instruction was that there be some evidence of diagnosis preceding or accompanying it. In other words, we were looking for purposeful, not random, efforts to provide for the learning needs of individuals. Interpreting our definition very generously, we were forced to conclude that there was no evidence of such individualization during the visits to some 90 of the classes — visits which were at least 45 minutes in length. The remainder provided some evidence but most of it was very limited and in only 5 of these was this provision judged to be extensive or considerable. There was little difference among the grade levels but, strangely, our group of special classes ranked very low on this criterion. Individual differences were presumed to be taken care of, apparently, by the practice of interclass grouping.

Much of what might be interpreted as individualizing instruction was a random process of calling on children for a response or following up a child's comment or observation as a kind of digression from the usual telling or questioning and answering kind of class activity. Even when the process met our definition, special attention to one child frequently occurred at the expense of others; other children were temporarily idled because alternative or continuing tasks were not provided for them. Very often, too, individualization was a quantitative thing, with the alternative task being more of the same rather than a differentiation in *kind* of work undertaken.

Related to the matter of individualizing instruction, we endeavored to pick up evidences regarding the teacher's awareness of a spread of ability or accomplishment among children in a class. In general, we were unsuccessful in doing so. Whether this was because teachers simply are not conscious of the range normally present in a class group, or because they are aware but are inept at providing for it, or because our observations were inadequate, is difficult to say.

## 1.8 Discipline and Control

The most frequently used techniques for disciplining and controlling individuals and groups were praise and verbal rewards, reminders of "appropriate" behavior, commands and directives, avoiding or ignoring the behavior by deliberate design, and threats. Praise and verbal rewards, together with reminders of standards or expected behavior, constituted the bulk of the items in our record; threats accounted for a small percentage of the total. On occasion, children were rewarded with juice or candy, names placed on an honor list, or some special privilege. Negative recognition occasionally took such forms as moving children from one place to another or removing them from the group, requiring that children lay their heads on the desks or sit in a corner, sending children outside or to the principal's office, and sarcasm. Sometimes, teachers made their disapproval known by pausing and looking directly at a child, drawing the class's attention to someone thought to be stepping out of line, raising the voice, scowling or frowning, touching the child, snapping fingers, and so on. In about 10 percent of the classrooms, there was little or no evidence of deliberate control mechanisms apart from involvement of pupils in the work under way. The data were not markedly different for grade levels. It should be noted, however, that reminders of appropriate behavior and commands ranked somewhat disproportionately high in our sample of special classes enrolling predominantly disadvantaged children.

The data in this category probably are more suspect than in any other. There is greater likelihood, we think, that pupils will behave better and that teachers will be more benign when visitors are in the classroom.

## 1.9 Pacing

This category refers to the rate at which each activity proceeded and followed each other. Rapid pacing described a hurried, rushed atmosphere, with children appearing to have inadequate time for each task. Moderate pacing was characterized by words in the anecdotal record such as busy, moving steadily but at a relaxed pace, enough time for the tasks at hand. Slow pacing characterized rooms in which time was wasted and sluggish performance often was the order of the day.

The overwhelming majority of classrooms appeared to be moderately paced, activities moving along in a rather relaxed, unhurried way. Classroom descriptions suggested that about 10 percent were fast paced and about 16 percent slow paced. Children and teachers in the sample were working at something most of the time, appearing neither to be in a hurry nor to dawdle. As would be expected, there were marked differences among children. There appeared not to be, however, marked differences among grade levels or categories of classes. The data here, too, must be regarded with considerable reservation, since persons under the gaze of a visitor are likely to make an appearance, at least, of being busy.

## 2. Independent Activities

Independent activities were defined as the tasks provided for or by the children to use by themselves while the teacher was engaged elsewhere with an individual or small group. We have noted previously, from data in the category on individualizing instruction, that there appeared to be a dearth of activities for other children when an effort was being made to provide separately for one child.

### 2.1 Provision and Use

Provision and use refers to the extent of provision of independent activities by the teacher and their amount of independent use by individuals or small groups. Our judgment of classrooms was based on the double-edged criterion of *both* availability and use.

Extensive provision and use of independent activities occurred only in kindergarten, and even here, in only about a sixth of the classes. However, extensive and moderate provision accounted for about a third of the entire sample of kindergarten classrooms. From the first grade through the third, provision for and use of independent activities was limited or virtually non-existent from an observer point of view. When activities other than the task at hand were being engaged in, they appeared to be very much like the regular academic activities and to be subject to teacher assignment or directive. At the time of our visits, about eight classes in fifteen had a single focus of instruction for all the children except that the children sometimes were divided into groups (as in reading) for the assigned tasks. In other words, no independent activities were visible in more than half of the classes.

## 2.2 Children's Involvement

The definition of involvement for independent activities was the same as for the instructional process as a whole (see p. 49). Just as provision and use of independent activities declined with upward progression through the grades, so did degree of involvement in them. The greatest incidence of high involvement was in the kindergarten; only one kindergarten class out of a total of twenty was rated as having low involvement. For the sample as a whole, a disproportionate number of the classes enrolling a high proportion of disadvantaged children was rated low on involvement.

It must be noted, of course, that the greater provision of independent activities at the kindergarten level provided also greater quantitative opportunity for high involvement in them. Nonetheless, the picture is clearly one of declining opportunity to participate in activities other than those under the immediate direction of teachers and declining involvement in whatever independent activities may be available as children progress upward from kindergarten through the third grade.

## 2.3 Degrees of Freedom

Closely related to the preceding is the degree of freedom for children to use the independent activities. A judgment of high degree of freedom indicated that children were permitted or even encouraged to move freely around the room, selecting for themselves activities in which to engage. At the other extreme, little or no such freedom existed; the work was assigned by the teacher to be done at children's desks.

In keeping with other findings in the independent activities category, the greatest freedom was exhibited in kindergarten classes and declined progressively in the higher grades. Interestingly, where there was at least moderate provision for independent activities and for their use, nearly half of the classes so rated allowed a great deal of freedom in selecting and pursuing them. The decision to provide for independent activities appeared to be accompanied by flexibility with respect to children being free to use them.

A visible difference between regular and disadvantaged classrooms appeared. A somewhat disproportionately large sample of so-called disadvantaged classes having independent activities available sharply restricted children's freedom in using them. The degree of control exercised by teachers in total class activities carried over into provisions for independent work.

### 2.4 Types

Under this rubric, we attempted only to list or describe the kinds of independent activities provided. In the kindergarten, painting and building with blocks, followed by crayon work and paper construction were the most popular independent activities. Occasionally, children occupied their time in a library center, with caring for plants, with puzzles, or in a playhouse. There were single examples of playing with clay, working with a number board, make-believe cooking, playing with toys, and so on.

In the first grade, reading (usually from library books) was the independent activity most frequently observed. Coloring with crayons ranked second. These were followed by infrequently observed activities such as working with puzzles, using worksheets, singing, playing with blocks or objects requiring manipulative skills, illustrating stories, etc. In the second grade, also, reading from library books was the most common independent activity but now follow-up work pertaining to regular lessons, including the use of workbooks, moved into second spot in regard to frequency. Behind these activities came drawing, copying and illustrating words, copying poems, and preparing short reports. The third grade appeared to be even more oriented to the regular academic program in provision for independent activities with reading, the use of workbooks, spelling, and various mathematics activities ranking high. There were no marked differences among types of classes in the sample.

Looking at the overall trend, toys, blocks, dolls, and puzzles virtually disappeared after the kindergarten level. Painting and art work, as independent activities, were strong in kindergarten and the first grade but were virtually nonexistent thereafter. Library books made their appearance in kindergarten and predominated in subsequent grades. Workbooks and various teacher-determined follow-up activities appeared in the first grade and were very much in evidence in the second and third. Independent activities clearly related to the language arts dominated independent classroom activity in first, second, and third grades.

## Curricular Provisions and Practices

Most of what one views in a classroom is instructional, in the broad sense of teachers teaching and students learning. Observers tend to observe the people and what they are doing. It is difficult to sort out data pertaining to other categories such as the one considered here, curricular provisions and practices.

We were concerned here, first, with materials and equipment which were obviously available; that is, they were in plain view to an observer. No attempt was made to look into cabinets and cupboards; nor was any effort made to assess the availability of instructional materials from some central source in the school district. Second, we wanted to find out about the curriculum as a source of instruction: where it came from, the assistance provided to teachers seeking to implement it, how teachers regarded this curriculum, and so on. In other words, we were trying to get data on the nature, intent, and adaptation of the curriculum drawn upon in teaching.

## 1. Materials and Equipment

The materials observed from room to room were very similar for the three grades, all of which differed from the kindergarten. Textbooks, virtually absent in the kindergarten, put in their appearance in the first grade and increased in number and variety in grades two and three. Just as textbooks increased abruptly after kindergarten, toys and games declined equally abruptly in the first and subsequent grades. First-grade textbooks were predominantly "readers" but there were, as well, some science texts, spellers, mathematics texts of the "old" and "new" variety, health or safety textbooks, music texts, and language books other than readers. Textbooks in the subject fields increased in number and variety in grades two and three.

All classes and grades (including the kindergarten) possessed what might be termed "library" books for guided and independent reading. But the number varied markedly from class to class, with less than one such book per child in evidence in some rooms and as many as five or six per child in others. Most of these were of the hardcover variety and ranged from picture books to informational and story books. Reference books were in short supply throughout; encyclopedias were visible in about a tenth of the classrooms and dictionaries in about one room in seven. Programmed materials were almost non-existent.

Although audio-visual equipment was used rarely during our visits, such equipment was available in many rooms. The items found most frequently were phonographs and records, tape recorders, abacuses, maps and globes. There was a scattering, at all levels, of movie and slide projectors, television sets, and, occasionally, overhead projectors. Maps and globes increased with the grade level. Conversely, the availability of art supplies declined as the grade level increased. In general, science materials were conspicuous by their absence, although many classes at all grade levels possessed plants, small rock collections, shell displays and living creatures of some kind (turtles, fish, hamsters, white rats, etc.). Likewise, there appeared to be a shortage of musical instruments, the few pianos and rhythm instruments of kindergarten and first-grade rooms declining in frequency in second and third grades.

Chalkboards were available in all rooms and either flannel boards or magnetic boards were at the lowest levels of schooling, becoming infrequent in grades two and three. Bulletin boards displayed both teachers' and children's work; commercial-type materials appeared with increasing frequency as the grades advanced; and the relationship between ongoing work and bulletin board displays became increasingly close with advancing grade level.

In regard to seating, the kindergarten rooms almost always provided some kind of table-and-chair arrangement, a pattern that faded until individual desks in rooms became equally uniform for the third grade. Similarly, the rug corners and reading circles of the first two years had virtually disappeared by the third and fourth.

The general picture is that of a play-like environment of the kindergarten, with considerable opportunity for freedom of movement and activity, giving way to a much more restricted and circumscribed academic environment thereafter. By the third grade, materials and seating arrangements suggest a passive, immobile pattern characterized by seatwork and total group activity under teacher direction.

## 2. The Instructional Curriculum

It proved rather difficult to determine the precise source of ideas for the instruction observed, especially in the kindergarten. At this level, local and district curriculum guides appeared to be the major source, although much of what the teachers were doing seemed to be based on their past experience and a rather uniform conception of what is "appropriate for kindergarten children." State guides loomed as a major source, along with county and local curriculum bulletins, at the first-grade level but here textbooks, too, played a strong part. In subsequent grades, textbooks outweighed all other sources in determining teaching and learning activities. In fact, the textbook was the immediate learning stimulus at the time of visitation in more than half the classes beyond the kindergarten. Almost uniformly, what might be called "standard" texts were in use — that is, the graded series revised and published year after year by a few large firms. Undoubtedly, some of the more recent revisions included attention to new curricular thrusts in the subject fields. But we found only a scattering of classrooms using new curriculum products in pure form, so to speak: in economics, science, and mathematics.

We endeavored to secure evidence of curriculum plans being developed by the school faculty as a whole or by committees of that faculty. We encountered only one example but, admittedly, evidence here was very difficult to obtain. Nonetheless, neither observations nor interviews with teachers and principals revealed faculties at work on curriculum problems and plans. In general, each class operated as an individual unit, taking curricular direction from textbooks, courses of study, and teachers' experience.

At all grade levels, teachers viewed themselves as having considerable flexibility with respect to curricular adaptation, especially with selecting activities to deal with bodies of content. Feelings of being restricted focused on expectations for coverage during a year, on time and subject schedules, and on lack of freedom to depart from required texts. Our impression from conversations with teachers was that they felt free to adopt and to enrich within a generally prescribed broad framework.

We had considerable difficulty getting insight into the amount and kind of help provided or available to teachers seeking to implement or develop a curriculum. Very few of the teachers appeared to be tied in directly to some source of help. Several were assisted by supervisors (we had expected a close relationship here, given the high incidence of supervisory personnel in the school districts represented); two or three were in some way involved with neighboring universities in collaborative projects; some participated in workshops or institutes designed to teach new content or method. With only a few exceptions, neither teachers as individuals nor schools as units participated in the various in-service activities that usually have been associated with curriculum reform projects in the United States.

## Significant Problems

We endeavored to determine, through interviews, the nature of the problems perceived by principals and teachers to be most pressing. We mentioned previously the difficulties inherent in seeking sustained, thoughtful interviews with elementary school teachers, given the nature of their teaching day and the structure of schools. Problems in interviewing the principals, however, were minimal. The results reported here are from 67 schools.

### 1. Principals' Perceptions

Given the nature of our sample, it is not surprising that three principals in ten placed at the top of their list of perceived problems a cluster pertaining to serving a harsh environment. They identified such specifics as parent apathy, lack of learning resources in the home, poverty, parental ignorance, children's lack of motivation, children's sensory deprivation, the need for school to provide food and clothing, limited parental proficiency in English, and on and on. One principal in five placed inadequate facilities at the top of his list: overcrowding, inflexibility, poor ventilation, inadequate play space, and limited equipment. Not surprisingly, many of these same principals and others identified as first or second on their list very closely related problems pertaining to the management of pupils in depressed communities: transiency, social and emotional difficulties, sheer resistance to the "press" of the school, particularly with respect to the learning fare, absenteeism and truancy.

About one principal in ten placed curricular and instructional problems at the top of his list: lack of appropriate materials (especially for disadvantaged children), inadequate time for coverage, undue expectations in relation to children's abilities, making the transition from traditional to modern approaches, inadequate provision for individual differences in commercial materials, etc. About the same number identified problems pertaining to teaching personnel; getting teachers to abandon outmoded programs and practices, mixing teachers with traditional as opposed to modern training, finding personnel of innovative bent, orienting new teachers, getting teachers to plan together or to work as a team, inducing the staff to effect change, keeping the staff up to date.

The remaining problems scattered widely, with few identifiable patterns. From one to three principals placed the following at or near the top of the list: community pressure, rigidity in central office policy, noneducational distractions surrounding school activity, no change in district expectations for the school following a shift in the pupil population, no kindergarten classes, difficulties in implementing plans of the central office, the strain of trying new things, and more.

It might be appropriate and useful to insert a subjective

observation about these discussions with principals. We had anticipated an outpouring of problems and plans, especially since the members of our visiting team were teachers struggling daily with the practical problems of keeping school and were, therefore, kindred spirits. It proved not difficult to pull out what might be called contextual problems: of the community, the homes, the school building, district policies, and the like. But conversation lagged when our interviewers sought to get at internal matters such as working with the staff for school improvement, providing for individual differences, and getting greater clarity with respect to school purpose and function. Most of the principals seemed unable to identify what the school needed most, plans under way to improve it, or problems viewed as first order of business in producing a better school. The principals, for the most part, were eager — hungry — to query our staff about what they saw as promising in various parts of the country but were inarticulate regarding the implications of these or any other ideas for their own schools.

## 2. Teachers' Perceptions

Whereas principals tended to identify community, home, district and total school problems, the teachers focused directly on children as they perceived them in the classroom. No other group of problems approached this one in frequency of mention. Specifics included the following: children with handicaps (mental, emotional, physical), general cultural deprivation, lack of motivation, inability to concentrate or communicate, apathy and passiveness, inability to follow directions, and behavior problems calling for discipline on the part of teachers. These last included unruliness of the class, restlessness, disruptions, giggling, and self-willed stubbornness. The magnitude and complexity of controlling an entire class was identified as a major problem by a substantial number of teachers.

The same community and home shortcomings identified

by principals were perceived by teachers in the context of the classroom: language background of parents, mobility, absenteeism, parental disinterest, fatigue caused by inadequate rest and nutrition, lack of readiness for school, and so on. Similarly, teachers referred to the lack of appropriate instructional materials, inadequate facilities, limited space and equipment, lack of time, and overcrowded classrooms. A relatively small number referred to difficulties encountered in seeking to make changes such as nongrading and team teaching and to provide a program relevant to individual pupil needs.

Teachers listed also a group of problems pertaining to their own adequacy, role, and support in teaching. Some expressed a desire for more decision-making authority, less lay involvement, more consultant help, greater assistance with problems such as teaching bilingual children and dealing with individual differences, less parental pressure, more freedom to depart from or adapt the curriculum, and specialized staff to deal with unique problems. A few mentioned a need for better prepared administrators, more flexible principals, and greater protection from administrators in regard to pressures, disruptions, and community activities. Several expressed a desire for better pre-service teacher education, with new teachers to be prepared on the job, and for a higher level of professional behavior.

The teachers, even more than the principals, were eager to discuss educational practices viewed elsewhere by our staff, readily taking advantage of invitations to breakfast or dinner in order to do so. (It was difficult to arrange for interviews during the school day.) It was in these discussions that the problems identified here usually came to the fore. But teachers rarely brought forward descriptions of what was being done or might be done about them in their schools. They appeared not to be at work on these problems in any cooperative, sustained way. As data reported earlier suggest, in-service activities tended to be individual, disparate, and unrelated to the pressing problems of individual schools. We found only a few instances of plans for coping as total school faculties with the problems which concerned them as individuals. In this connection, data revealed that four of the principals were providing strong leadership for the improvement of curriculum and instruction. Our staff reported evidences of this leadership in the classrooms visited; they found a cohesive relationship between the school improvement effort under way as perceived by the principal and what the teachers were doing or said they were trying to do in the classroom.

## Change and Innovation

One of several motivations for this study was a desire to find out whether some of the more innovative educational practices recommended in recent years actually were finding their way into the schools. For this reason, among others, we endeavored to select schools enrolling a high proportion of culturally disadvantaged children, schools considered typical, and schools considered to be innovative. We assumed that this first group of schools, eligible for special federal funds, increasingly would be moving toward new and perhaps innovative practices.

Although we insisted that our team of observers seek data on change and innovation, we assiduously avoided both a definition of innovation and a check list of practices considered in advance to be innovative. Instead, we took three approaches to the problem of identifying newer thrusts: encouraging teachers and principals to report any practice they considered to be out of the ordinary, asking our staff to list anything observed that they considered to be innovative, and requesting information on the implementation of popular innovations such as nongrading and team teaching. Practices considered to be innovative by some school faculties would be assumed by others to be standard. To repeat, it must be remembered that some of the schools were selected for us as being innovative.

The practices cited ranged widely; there were few patterns. One cluster pertained to the organization and management of the school, another to curriculum and instruction. Thirteen schools reported preschool programs, usually of the Head Start variety, all supported by federal funds. Fourteen had nonprofessional aides assisting the regular teachers. Six were in the process of introducing their first kindergarten classes. Fifteen schools maintained special classes for exceptional children: four for the gifted, three for mentally retarded children, three for emotionally disturbed, one to provide advanced placement, and one each for blind, speech-defective, deaf, or physically handicapped children. The principals of nine schools reported departures from report cards and the use of parent-teacher conferences for reporting pupil progress. Five schools held meetings with various specialists in order to provide teachers with stimulating ideas.

A few schools had established or were in the process of establishing new patterns of school or classroom organization. A few schools practiced a system of exchanging children among teachers for part or all of the day, a system which appeared to us to be departmentalization. Sixteen schools reported team teaching for periods ranging from an hour to the entire day, but there were enormous variations in what was being called team teaching. On occasion, the team teaching label was applied to a practice of turning the class over to specialists for one or more periods of the day. Likewise, the 15 schools reporting to be nongraded applied the label to a variety of practices, including interclass grouping by homogeneity in ability or achievement. Often, there was a vast difference between the implications of the label applied and the observations of our staff who frequently concluded that the practice claimed simply did not exist in any reasonably recognizable form. In only a few instances were the buildings especially designed for these organizational practices.

A substantial number (19 schools) sought in one way or another to expand the materials and other instructional resources available to children. Beyond this concentration, however, efforts to introduce something new into the instructional effort defied classification and generalization. Three schools had a foreign language program; one taught English as a second language to foreign-speaking children; three reported individualized reading programs; three used the mathematics materials of special curriculum projects; two used new science materials; two used experimental social studies materials; several used reading materials which departed from the standard textbook series; and nine schools were using materials prepared in local projects.

Many of the schools in deprived areas used federal grants to extend the school program in various ways. Eleven provided after-school study programs. Three reported summer programs designed to assist underachievers in one way or another. Our staff noted that these programs, where observed, extended the school program described on preceding pages. They tended not to be trying different things in different ways.

Occasionally, we visited schools which were involved in some larger experimental project. One participated as one of ten project schools in an effort to improve language development through filmstrips, tape recorders, and listening centers. One had joined six others in a federally-financed experiment comparing six ways of teaching reading. Two participated in a study designed to determine and evaluate the effects of team teaching.

Individual teachers reported a variety of classroom practices which they considered to be promising, unique, or innovative. The largest cluster pertained to creating a more open, flexible classroom environment designed to encourage individual progress. Specific practices cited ranged from giving children more freedom to pedagogical techniques for controlling children to patterns of deliberately homogeneous or heterogeneous grouping. Several noted the advantages of having special classes in the school for children with learning and other disabilities.

## Some Concluding Perceptions

We have mentioned that cohesive, comprehensive plans or programs of school improvement transcending most or all of the staff, principal and teachers alike, did not come to our attention. Four schools approached a sense of common commitment, with principals exerting vigorous leadership and a large percentage of their staffs appearing to share the goals and concerns articulated by these principals. In general, however, we were unable to substantiate claims of school-wide effort through classroom observations and conversations with teachers and principals. Projects usually appeared to be "tacked on" rather than integrated into the fabric of the school. Most involved a classroom or two and seemed not to be shared or discussed by the faculty as a whole or by segments of it.

A very subjective but nonetheless general impression of those who gathered and those who studied the data was that some of the highly recommended and publicized innovations of the past decade or so were dimly conceived and, at best, partially implemented in the schools claiming them. The novel features seemed to be blunted in the effort to twist the innovation into familiar conceptual frames or established patterns of schooling. For example, team teaching more often than not was some pattern of departmentalization and nongrading looked to be a form of homogeneous grouping. Similarly, the new content of curriculum projects tended to be conveyed with the baggage of traditional methodology.

An interesting and perhaps significant discrepancy between the perceptions of our staff and some of the teachers and principals showed up rather frequently in the record. Since we did not set out to gather data on this discrepancy (or for that matter, with an alertness to its possible existence), any attempt to quantify this finding would be meaningless or misleading. It is clear, however, that a substantial number of principals and teachers perceived ongoing instruction to be characterized by some of our "reasonable expectations" when members of our staff did not. They claimed individualization of instruction, use of a wide range of instructional materials, a sense of purpose, group processes, and inductive or discovery methods when our records showed little or no evidence of them. In the "comment" section of the record, our staff frequently noted the relatively high-level claims of teachers and principals in contrast to their own, discouraging low perceptions. There appeared to be little or no relationship between teachers' and principals' perceptions and what our staff recorded as reality. That is, a principal or teacher might claim a high or low level of individualizing instruction but this in no way forecast our own conclusions. When evidence on this point is in the record, however, our perceptions are generally and substantially lower than those of both principals and teachers. These perceptions and the discrepancy between them are further explored in Chapter Five.

## Notes

1. See, for example, National Education Association, *The Principals Look at the Schools: A Status Study of Selected Instructional Practices* (Washington, D.C., 1962).

2. Ned A. Flanders, *Teacher Influence, Pupil Attitudes and Achievement* (Cooperative Research Project no. 397, U.S. Office of Education. Minneapolis, Minn: University of Minnesota Press, 1960); Ned A. Flanders, *Teacher Influence, Pupil Attitudes and Achievement* (OE-25040, Cooperative Research Monograph no. 12. Washington, D.C.: U.S. Government Printing Office, 1965).

3. See, for example, John I. Goodlad, "The Organizing Center in Curriculum Theory and Practice," *Theory into Practice,* vol. I, October, 1962, pp. 215-221; M. Frances Klein, "Evaluation of Instruction: Measurement of Cognitive Behavior as Defined by the Taxonomy of Educational Objectives" (Ed.D. dissertation, University of California, Los Angeles, 1965); Robert M. McClure, "Procedures, Processes, and Products in Curriculum Development," (Ed.D. dissertation, University of California, Los Angeles, 1965).

4. Benjamin S. Bloom, ed. *Taxonomy of Educational Objectives; the Classification of Educational Goals.* Handbook I: *The Cognitive Domain* (New York: Longmans, Green and Company, 1956); David R. Krathwohl, Benjamin S. Bloom, and Bertram B. Masia, *Taxonomy of Educational Objectives; the Classification of Educational Goals.* Handbook II: *Affective Domain* (New York: David McKay Company, Inc., 1964).

# Chapter Four

# Perspectives on Schooling

Our conclusions regarding the set of ten reasonable expectations for schooling in the United States, presented in Chapter One, can now be seen in full context. These conclusions are based on observations in 150 classrooms of 67 schools selected from major population centers of the country.

## Educational Objectives and School Function

At the outset we had difficulty agreeing on comprehensive categories and developing instruments for gathering data. Our trial check list included a category pertaining to educational objectives. More often than not, the items here were marked "no evidence." This proved to be the result, also, with use of the anecdotal technique finally decided upon. In general, our observers had grave difficulty gathering evidence regarding what teachers were endeavoring to accomplish in the classroom apart from coverage of topics selected largely from courses of study and textbooks. If there were central concepts or children's needs and interests guiding the selection of specific learning activities, they escaped our attention. Likewise, we had difficulty relating verbal rewards and other teacher recognition of approved behavior to some larger sense of direction. We are forced to conclude that the vast majority of teachers in our sample was oriented more to a drive for coverage of certain material than to a reasonably clear perception of behavior sought in their pupils.

Likewise, from conversations with teachers and principals, we were unable to identify a sense of direction or priorities for each individual school. Although there often was a core of agreement regarding the problems faced, these usually were contextual in character — that is, problems of conditions of home and community to be taken into account in planning the school program. It is our belief that, given admittedly complex situational conditions, the proper educational response is, "Given this community, these homes, language disabilities, and all the rest, how should the school respond? What are our educational priorities?" But, except for a few instances, we encountered neither this kind of thinking nor ongoing staff efforts or even embryonic plans to cope with what obviously were problems of great magnitude. As we have noted and will comment on further, classroom programs were remarkably similar from school to school, regardless of location and local realities. We conclude that most of the schools visited were oriented to some generally accepted concept of what school is (a school is a school is a school) and not to an ongoing inquiry into either group or individual learning needs of specific children in particular communities. There was, in fact, a notable absence of total staff or small group dialogue about education in general or school plans and prospects.

## Learning How To Learn

Most adults are familiar with early school instruction that was largely didactic — that is, the conveying of information. We learned many things *for sure:* that there are 92 elements (*sic*), that the molecule is the smallest piece of matter (*sic*), and that these are the capitals of certain (now non-existent) countries. In recent years, presumably, much of this sort of thing has been replaced by inductive learning. Students inquire, discover for themselves, conclude that fact is a man-made, temporary phenomenon, and endeavor to learn how to learn. But this was not our finding.

The instructional environment of the classes we visited, more in grades one through three than in the kindergarten, were characterized by telling, teachers' questioning individual children in group settings, and an enormous amount of seemingly quite routine seatwork. Rather than probing, seeking, inquiring, children were predominantly responding and covering. Even when using the materials of curriculum projects presumably emphasizing "discovery" methods, pupils appeared bent on covering the content of textbooks, workbooks, and supplementary reading material. We do not wish to imply that all instruction in schools should be of the inductive sort. But we do conclude that telling and questioning were the predominant characteristics of instruction in our sample of classrooms.

## Subject Matter

Given twentieth-century stress on the role of interest in learning, one of our expectations was that the subject matter of instruction would have considerable intrinsic appeal for youngsters. Our finding in this respect is more toward neutrality than either unkindled enthusiasm or stultifying boredom. Perhaps it would be fair to say, given our own reactions to this subject matter, that children and teachers alike were making the most of it: talking, reading, and writing about it and occasionally moving out from it in tasks of building, drawing, or singing but the subject matter itself seemed not to go far in stimulating creativity.

For our part, we were struck with the dullness, abstractness, and lack of variety in the learning fare. Perhaps this was because of the heavy reading and language orientation of the programs. We, all of us in the education enterprise, seem strangely unable to provide stimulating content for this childhood phase of schooling which is now geared so closely to processes of reading, writing, and listening. Even some of the more experimental efforts to replace the homogenized content and mechanical phraseology of standard reading series with more virile stuff have ended up looking surprisingly like the originals. Using color to convey our impressions, the subject matter of ongoing instruction was done more in sepia than in technicolor.

Our conclusions, then, are a mixed bag. On one hand we conclude that the subject matter coming into the classrooms we visited was surprisingly uniform from room to room, machine-made in quantities sufficient for all children, generally lacking in power to hold or grip, often unimaginative in verbal or artistic portrayal, and usually packaged in one rather than several modes of presentation. On the other hand, we conclude that teachers and children were adapting to it reasonably well, appearing for the most part to be neither enthusiastic nor unduly bored.

## Instructional Materials

Visiting the publishers' booths at an educational convention, perusing the counters of the children's section in bookstores, or reading audio-visual catalogues leads one to conclude that this is, indeed, the golden age of educational materials. But our visits left us with an entirely different impression so far as entry into the schools is concerned. Textbooks and workbooks dominated the teaching-learning process. As noted in the detailed account of findings, we saw some movie projectors, tape recorders, record players, filmstrip projectors, globes, maps, encyclopedias, and dictionaries. But these were, in our judgment, in short supply for the schools of an affluent society. Further, we seldom saw them in use — hardly ever by children individually and of their own self-directed volition. Toys, games, and manipulatable learning devices virtually disappeared after kindergarten. We saw few teacher-made or child-made devices, little construction employing saw and hammer, few field trips or preparations for them, little exploration of the outdoors or of fantasy. Are we losing our touch with the world of real things? Our ability to create, to make things with our hands? Are these matters being taken care of outside of school? Is school to be concerned only with the academic?

We conclude that the prime medium of instruction in our sample of schools was the textbook, supported by textbook-like related reading and workbooks. We conclude, also, that in these schools, at least, the much-vaunted systems approach to instructional materials, in which an array of media is used, lies perhaps in the future but is not characteristic of the present. If one dare generalize beyond the sample, this is not yet the era of the electronic classroom wherein an arsenal of instructional materials lies ready to respond to the call or touch of pupils and teachers.

## Individual Differences

If our staff of visiting teachers was at any time shaken up by elements of the task undertaken, it was in response to their search for individualized instruction. The importance of and ways to individualize instruction have dominated educational discourse for years. Principals and teachers alike spoke frequently of individual needs, individual differences, and provisions for both during conversations with them. Some teachers spoke of new thrusts in their classrooms designed to provide more effectively for individuality. But the instruction we observed was, in our judgment, overwhelmingly group-oriented.

The dominant teaching-and-questioning type of instruction usually was conducted with the entire class. When classes were broken into groups, the activity was reading, with one group reading to the teacher, one reading independently (often with common materials), and one group doing seatwork related to the preceding or forthcoming lesson. Seatwork assignments were common to large numbers of children, the quick usually finishing and turning to other work, the slow hardly ever completing the assignment. Rarely were children engaged in self-initiated and self-directed small group or individual activity; rarely were children engaged in activity lying outside of the daily scope of the classroom. These generalizations apply less well to the kindergarten where several activities often proceeded simultaneously and where youngsters sometimes worked on matters of more spontaneous and individual interest.

Our data lead to the firm conclusion that the overwhelming majority of our 150 classrooms—in organization, subject matter, materials, and mode of instruction—were geared to group norms and expectancies rather than to individual differences in learning rate and need. Judging from our sample, childhood schooling is more vanilla than pistachio or neopolitan.


## Principles of Learning and Instruction

In our trial check list, we sought to identify use of those principles of learning and teaching which, we assumed, were taught in education courses and carried to some degree by teachers into the classroom. As with the category of educational objectives, trial runs tended to produce "no evidence." Similarly with the extensive anecdotal records, we simply were unable to pull out of the material pieces of data to suggest that principles of learning were being used extensively and effectively as teaching tools.

We commented earlier on the importance of intrinsic motivation and have passed sober judgment regarding the apparent low level of it inherent in much of the materials and subject matter employed. We failed to turn up much evidence regarding teachers' efforts to remedy this deficiency through use of perhaps less desirable but nonetheless productive extrinsic motivation. It seemed to us, also, that praise and verbal rewards (positive reinforcement) often were perfunctorily given and not clearly designed to attract a child's attention to the close relationship between his effort and some goal or model. Our inability to identify behaviors being either reinforced or extinguished appeared to be a corollary of our inability to identify agreed-upon goals or some general sense of direction. At very specific levels of instruction (working with a small reading group, for example), teachers appeared not to be diagnosing learning difficulties and then moving in or following up with pinpointed intervention strategies.

Although we saw little application of learning principles in any specific sense — that is, in diagnosis and subsequent pedagogical response to learning deficiency or success — we observed substantial supportive behavior on the part of teachers. In general, they were rather warm and encouraging, apparently seeking to establish rapport rather than to create barriers or gulfs between pupils and themselves.

We conclude, then, that the teachers we observed, either by deliberate intent or a naturally positive attitude toward children, tended to support their pupils through encouragement and warmth in their overt behavior. But we must conclude, also, that most of them appeared to be unaware of the learning principles provided by psychologists, saw little use for them, or simply were unable to put them to use in teaching.


## Classroom Interaction

Findings regarding classroom interaction patterns overlap and coincide with findings regarding instruction. With teachers in the dominant role of telling and questioning, it is not surprising that interaction between and among children was limited. Frequently, our staff plotted these patterns; anecdotal records always included data on them. The prevailing pattern was teacher to child, child to teacher, teacher to another child, child back to teacher, and over again. Or, it was a more random pattern, with a child responding to a question thrown out to all by the teacher, the teacher continuing, and either the pattern repeating or children injecting comments and questions as the teacher proceeded. As reported, small-group learning either provided individual activity in common work or set the teacher up as the dominant figure in the same kind of teacher-child interaction. The most random kind of discussion usually followed a film or report. But, again, a child's comment almost always followed or initiated a teacher's comment.

There was a paucity of instances wherein a small group appeared to be planning its topic for instruction, assigning responsibilities, and moving forward with limited teacher guidance. Rarely did we find several such groups operating simultaneously with the teacher serving as a kind of consultant. The teacher was the source, supervisor, and evaluator of almost all classroom activity.

We conclude that, for the most part, the teachers in our sample were not relying on children as the instigators and planners of classroom activity; that child-to-child interaction only occasionally was characteristic of classrooms; and that these young children were gaining only very limited experience with the techniques and self-discipline of group intercourse.

## Norms, Standards, and Evaluation

The tests being used in the schools were almost uniformly of the grade-norm variety and overwhelmingly in the tradition of group achievement and intelligence testing. Criterion-referenced tests — that is, tests designed to get at a child's actual status with respect to some criterion of performance— were virtually non-existent. Some of the tests used, as in reading, might have been used to diagnose a child's competence in broad areas of performance but, usually, they were not employed in this way. Rather, scores were translated into grade equivalents and entered on class record sheets. Thus, the visible information available was that a child scored at grade 1.9 in this, 2.2 in something else, 2.9 in that, and 2.6 over-all. But the record sheet did not reveal whether this child had problems with the grapheme-phoneme translation, in composing sentences, or with the commutative law. So far as tests, records, and interpretations were concerned, individuality was washed out by the universality of grade standards.

As an aside, it must be admitted that tests for individual diagnosis of performance are hard to come by, although such tests increasingly are being constructed. Even if they were easily accessible, however, it would appear from our sample that overcoming grade and group norms in seeking to use them properly constitutes a formidable obstacle.

We found few instances of classrooms in which the ceilings and floors of expectancy had been widened to take care of the realities of a class group, even in schools claiming to be nongraded, as reported previously. Instead, efforts to nongrade, more often than not, went in the direction of seeking homogeneity in expectancy, attainment, materials, and the like, frequently with an eye to bringing pupils up to grade standard. Nongrading, by contrast, assumes heterogeneity in any group no matter how small or how established, seeks to draw attention to pupil variability, and functions meaningfully only when materials and activities are designed to meet individual needs and are not dictated by the grade. It appeared to us that most of the so-called nongraded schools were endeavoring to tack nongrading onto the existing structure instead of exploring the full implications of a new structure.

We conclude that the schools and classrooms of our sample, with very few exceptions, were committed in actual functioning, if not in intent, to graded expectations, graded standards, graded norms and the characteristics of curriculum, materials, and instruction that normally accompany the well-established, traditional graded school. There were strong desires and a few efforts to do otherwise. But, in general, the concepts were rather dimly understood, the logistics appeared formidable, and the sheer magnitude of simultaneously keeping school and changing it were discouraging to the staff. We encountered very little resistance to the desirability of the changes implied. The overriding problem expressed was lack of time; the persistent question was "How do we do it?"


## Human Resources and
## the Locus for Schooling

The schools we visited made very little use of human resources other than those full-time teachers assigned to the buildings. In general, one teacher served all or most of the needs of a single classroom, although student teachers and, much less frequently, community aides sometimes were present. Supervisors and special resource personnel from the central office rarely were seen by us; our queries failed to produce evidence that they were frequently in the classroom. In those instances when they came into the classroom, it appeared that they took over a special class, or group. When teachers moved about from room to room, it was to "trade" subjects, not to work as part of a planned team activity. Although team teaching was claimed by a substantial number of schools, we found only occasional instances of team planning, initiating, teaching, and evaluating. Very rarely did a team include paraprofessional, sub-professional, or part-time personnel. And rarely was the team activity carried on for more than an hour or two of the day.

It was exceedingly unusual to find a classroom group that ventured, as a whole or in part, into the larger community surrounding the school or that brought a human learning resource (doctor, lawyer, artist, plumber, dancer, scientist) into the room. The children came into the building in the morning and stayed there throughout the school schedule. Likewise, they came into classrooms and, except for some movement to other classrooms, remained there.

We conclude that education, in the schools we visited, was something that took place for daily stretches of from three hours (many kindergartens) to six hours; that was conducted almost entirely in the place called "school"; and that was confined to one or more classrooms. Further, we conclude that the teaching was done almost exclusively by full-time teachers, or substitutes like them, employed specifically for this purpose. In these early grades, both children and individual teachers associated as one self-contained cell in the building, carrying on only limited commerce with the inhabitants of neighboring cells.

## Curricular Balance

Traditionally, the early school years have been dominated by language activities (reading, writing, spelling, and listening) topped off by number work. But national interests and emphases of recent years would suggest considerable school expansion into other curricular areas. We did not find in the schools visited the breadth in the curriculum we had anticipated.

As expected, language activities dominated throughout, becoming increasingly academic and structured beyond the kindergarten level. Teaching in mathematics, more than any other field, reflected new emphases so far as content was concerned. As noted earlier, however, it appeared to us that "old pedagogy" was being used to implement whatever "new math" was being attempted.

Although social studies, science, art, music, and health appeared on teachers' schedules, little time was allocated and all of these appeared to be seriously neglected in the classroom. We encountered social studies lessons but these appeared frequently to be designed for further practice in the language arts, rather than for developing understanding in social science concepts. Similarly, drawing, crayoning, and painting, when in evidence, tended to be supplementary to reading (for example, drawing something seen in or envisioned from a story). Music activity usually was singing, frequently as a recreational break or as a way of beginning or concluding the day. We were both surprised and disappointed at the paucity of science instruction, the dearth of materials for doing things in science, and in our judgment, the superficial level of teaching science. Clearly, these teachers lacked the background and insights needed for effective science teaching.

We conclude that the curriculum of these four early years was overwhelmingly tilted toward the language arts to the apparent neglect of almost all other fields. Further, we conclude that both the pedagogy and the perspective with respect to these other fields was such that their inherent nature — their structure and method as realms of human inquiry — were obscured rather than illuminated.


## Additional Conclusions and Impressions

In the process of checking out the ten reasonable expectations we set forth at the outset, we observed and gathered data on additional aspects of early schooling. In Chapter Two, we described the problems involved in getting agreement on categories by means of which to describe schooling in some comprehensive way. Some of these categories, growing out of staff dialogue, now provide a check list by means of which to pull out a few conclusions and impressions not included in preceding paragraphs.

It will be recalled that the average age of the buildings visited was twenty-five years. Only one in three was of the one-story variety. In general, the buildings were drab in appearance, often to the point of being formidably unattractive. There were few trees, boulders, ravines, and other departures from the leveled ground and large areas of blacktop or concrete. The concrete and drabness diminished in traveling to outlying areas where the "leveled look" persisted but was more often broken by landscaping. Occasionally, too, there were new, bungalow-type buildings with bright doors and hallways. The city schools were very much like their harsh surroundings; suburban schools like their softer settings. Certainly, these schools were not countervailing to their large environment. In fact, they tended to be among the least attractive and prepossessing structures of their milieu. Rather than being the "educational palaces" one sometimes hears about, these schools appeared to be artifacts of a society that didn't care.

Inside, most of the schools visited were of eggcrate design, with self-contained classrooms down both sides of hallways. Corridors provided little inkling of classroom activity. Except for occasional display cases in entry halls, evidences of children's creativity were rarely in view: no projects ongoing (perhaps because of fire regulations) and only occasionally art work on the walls. It is of interest to contrast this with many Infant Schools (enrolling five-, six-, and seven-year-olds) in England: the entry hall often sets an art, music, or literature theme for the whole school; children's products line the hallways; and classroom activities spew out into all available nooks and crannies as well as to the outdoors.

In the classrooms, the teachers almost always were immediately visible, usually in front of the room and usually addressing or questioning the entire class or a subgroup of it. Children usually were seated at desks or tables, moving about only occasionally and rarely clustered in small working groups. Again, by contrast, teachers in many English Infant Schools tend not to be immediately identifiable, frequently they are on the level of the children, sitting or working with them. The impression gleaned from our sample was one of order, neatness, quietness, and immobility. These generalizations apply equally, we conclude, whether classrooms were in schools classified for us as ordinary, innovative, or disadvantaged. We found no marked differences, but classroom freedom appeared to be somewhat more restricted for this last group. Also, kindergarten classes deviated somewhat toward greater movement and flexibility. Kindergarten teachers were less obvious in the classroom than were other teachers.

We have commented on the "sameness" of activity from room to room and on what appeared to be a great deal of routine. We were struck also by the sameness of activities within any given room, whether or not designed for enrichment or individual supplementation to the regular program. We rarely saw an abrupt turnaround from the kind of instruction we have described to vigorous constructing, playacting, or dancing. Independent activities, when provided, meant more of the same reading (but with different books), writing, and coloring. Is some stereotype of schooling so built into our culture that it virtually shapes the entire enterprise, discouraging or even destroying deviations from it?

Interestingly, our data suggested some ambiguity at the kindergarten level regarding the image of what school should be and do. On several matters pertaining to teacher domination, control, independent activities, and self-direction of pupils, there was a bimodal distribution of classrooms; that is, kindergarten classes were disproportionately grouped at both ends of the total distribution of classes. Although the kindergartens, in general, appeared to be more open, flexible, and permissive than the others, a block of them deviated markedly toward a strong academic orientation and marked teacher control. It would appear that some kindergarten teachers saw kindergarten as providing opportunities for socialization, play, and choice-making, and accompanied this point of view with a permissive view of children's behavior. Another group saw it as "preparation for school," with a strong emphasis on academic work, especially reading and reading readiness activities, and accompanied this viewpoint with a rather strong measure of teacher control and domination.

In regard to this matter of control, our data suggested somewhat less freedom for children and the use of firmer control mechanisms in classrooms enrolling large percentages of environmentally disadvantaged children. This was so at all four grade levels. Unfortunately, we gathered no evidence regarding allocation of teachers to schools and so do not know the extent to which teachers of like background were assigned to these classrooms. It would be important and interesting to know, for example, whether behavioral expectations and control patterns change when predominantly black classes are taught by black rather than by white teachers.

It will be recalled that, in general, our findings were similar from classroom to classroom, regardless of any prejudgment by the school system as to the school's population or innovative character. But one striking difference with respect to the disadvantaged classes fell out. As would be expected, given the recommendations of specialists studying the learning deficiencies of harsh environment boys and girls, language activities dominated their instruction in kindergarten and the first grade. Surprisingly, however, these dropped off rapidly afterward until they were significantly less frequent in the second and third grades. Further, the range of learning activities narrowed at about the same rate: rhythms and dance, physical education, and concrete kinds of learnings were both less common than they had been in kindergarten and first grade and markedly less frequent than in the second and third-grade classes of the larger sample. Ironically, we know that language stimulation must be kept up if ongoing environmental deprivation is to be compensated for. Also, it is believed that both concrete learnings and emphasis on motor coordination are exceedingly important aspects of education for disadvantaged children — for that matter, all children.

Two findings pertaining to grouping practices are of interest. We noted that differentiated instruction designed to provide for individual differences seldom was in evidence in the sample of "special" classes. Children already had been assigned to these classes because of their giftedness, achievement, or disability. Similarly, such provision appeared to be limited when interclass grouping had occurred; that is, when children from several classes were re-grouped and assigned on the basis of some criterion of homogeneity, usually achievement. This pair of findings raises the intriguing question as to whether teachers assume that individual needs are more or less taken care of by such grouping practices. Do they often assume, for example, that placing 30 slow readers together for instruction takes care of a considerable portion of their need for individualized attention? If so, this would explain, at least partially, why various patterns of interclass grouping have failed to produce spectacular results in pupil achievement and adjustment. In general, grouping reduces heterogeneity in pupil characteristics very little and the need for individual attention not at all.

We conclude with two impressions regarding the majority of teachers in our sample. First, it would appear that neither pre-service nor in-service teacher education programs have provided them with the precise pedagogical understandings and skills required for diagnosing and remedying the learning programs and needs of individual pupils. Perhaps this explains, at least in part, why mass teaching of groups prevails. Or, it may be that the persistence of mass, total class teaching inhibits individual approaches and prevents the development of techniques geared to individuality.

Second, it would appear that teachers are very much alone in their work. It is not just a matter of being alone, all *all* alone with children in a classroom cell, although this is a significant part of their aloneness. Rather, it is the feeling — and in large measure the actuality — of not being supported by someone who knows about their work, is sympathetic to it, wants to help and, indeed, does help. This is, in part, an unhappy consequence of the inviolate status of the classroom and the assumed autonomy of the teacher in it. This aloneness becomes poignant in the face of problems which, clearly, cannot be solved by the individual teacher alone.

# Chapter Five

# Toward the Reconstruction of Schooling

Our findings are not markedly different from those of others who have taken the time to look in some depth at what goes on behind the classroom door.[1] Early reactions to a brief summary of these findings[2] suggest that many schools in the country differ with respect to some of the scene we have described. A highly suggestive pattern has emerged, however, which we assume applies to a large number of schools.

## Emerging Patterns

One conclusion stands out clearly: many of the changes we have believed to be taking place in schooling have not been getting into classrooms; changes widely recommended for the schools over the past 15 years were blunted on school and classroom door. Second, schools and classrooms were marked by a sameness regardless of location, student enrollment, and "typing" as provided initially to us by an administrator.

Third, there seemed to be a considerable discrepancy between teachers' perceptions of their own innovative behavior and the perceptions of observers. The teachers sincerely thought they were individualizing instruction, encouraging inductive learning, involving children in group processes, and so on. Fourth, "special," supplementary, and enrichment activities and practices differed very little from "regular" classroom activities. Fifth, general or specific classroom goals were not identifiable to observers. Instruction was general in character and not specifically directed to diagnosed needs, progress, and problems of individual children. Teachers shot with a shotgun, not a rifle. Sixth, the direction being pursued by the school as a whole was equally obscure or diffused.

Seventh, there appeared not to be a critical mass of teachers, parents, and others working together toward developing either a sense of direction or solutions to school-wide problems concerning them. Eight parallels number seven: school personnel appeared to be very much alone in their endeavors. Principals tended to remain in offices and hallways and not to intrude on sacred classroom ground in any direct way. Teachers, although alone and presumably free to teach in their classrooms, appeared to be bound to a common conception of what school is and should be.

It is interesting to place this scene against the backdrop of how aspects of the larger educational enterprise have been and are conducted in the United States (see Chapter One). In so doing, perhaps we will gain some insights as to why truly exciting proposals conceived and even developed by project staffs appear to lose much of their innovative character in any broad-scale attempt to implement them; why the form and not the substance of seemingly powerful proposals for change is what the schools embrace; and why the heat of educational change is so puny in comparison with the smoke. Comprehensive reasons, no doubt, will escape us but perhaps some useful hypotheses will emerge.

On the basis of our evidence, we are not prepared to say with many of the so-called romantic critics that the schools are dehumanizing institutions, devoid of teachers who care for children and of programs designed for their welfare.[3] That there are such schools has been rather extensively reported in recent years. Our concern, rather, is that there appeared to be in the schools we visited a rather uniform "flatness"; a lack of excitement, joy, and enthusiasm; an excess of routine and vicarious rather than direct experience; a limited variety of ways for doing things. A large part of schooling always has been like this. There are those, presumably, who would conclude that what we observed was neither damaging nor bad; just school as it is and probably will continue to be.

We view the situation differently. Although what we saw may not be damaging for most or many children, it simply is not good enough. If our sample can be taken as a reasonable basis for judgment, our elementary schools are not exciting learning centers, using a variety of pedagogical techniques, subject matter, materials, and activities designed to promote effective learning in most pupils. Especially, they seem not to be organized and conducted so as to assure a love of learning and development of the skills needed for lifelong-learning. This is particularly the case for school clientele coming from homes where intellectual pursuits are limited in nature or not valued. The schools appear unwilling or unable (or both) to break away from their essentially middleclass orientation.

Perhaps the most telling observation about our educational system is that there is not, below the level of intense criticism and endless recommendations for improvement, any effective structure by means of which countervailing ideas and models may be pumped in and developed to the point of becoming real alternatives. Stated conversely, the system is geared to self-preservation, not to self-renewal. Almost everything that follows is virtually an elaboration of this overarching condition.

## Insights into the Educational Enterprise

In our judgment, the patterns of primary schooling we observed do not constitute desirable models for so-called preschool education. To attempt to extend such patterns downward or to get children ready for them is a mistake. The inherent danger in the current upsurge of interest in educating the young child is that planning and programming will be motivated and even justified on the basis of readying him for school and improving his performance there. These are the motivations and justifications implied by the term "preschool." Planning and conducting educational programs for three-, four-, and five-year-olds presents a fresh opportunity which soon will be lost if the preschool syndrome prevails. Such programs must be planned from the bottom up and not provided through a process of slippage downward from existing schooling.

We recommend the creation of an early childhood unit of schooling, embracing a period beginning on or soon after the third birthday and continuing through approximately the fifth year of life. The purposes motivating and justifying it would have little to do with "preparing for school" but very much to do with developing healthy young humans in every aspect of development. It is assumed that the learning activities provided in such a phase of schooling would contribute, indeed, to later success in reading and a host of other accomplishments. But the substance and the context at all times would be "appropriate, meaningful education now," not preparation for something yet to come. We would hope that such a point of view and learning opportunities to accompany it would then slide up to infiltrate the years of schooling described on preceding pages.

One major effort to improve the schools has focused on the content and processes of learning and teaching the curriculum. For more than a dozen years, the National Science Foundation has provided substantial support to selected projects in precollegiate mathematics and science. A more recent and diffused effort to update and enrich the curriculum has been under way in the social sciences, arts, and humanities. First-rate scholars have participated in this rather broad-scale effort for at least brief periods of time.

The early leaders of this curriculum reform movement recognized the magnitude of the task of retraining teachers. Teachers were brought into the curriculum-building process for substantial periods of time, becoming true partners in the enterprise, with commitments from the school district to facilitate their new learnings, from the teachers to try out new methods and materials, and from the projects to provide follow-up services. All of this is expensive and time-consuming — but likely to make an impact. Later efforts were much less thorough. Teachers usually were provided with relatively brief orientations and, often, with no follow-up help other than that provided by teachers' manuals. Many received no orientation whatsoever. It is not surprising that the form and not the substance of many of the promising enterprises for curricular change is what found its way into the classroom. In our visits to schools, we saw new content twisted into conventional learning and teaching procedures. We most certainly failed to find a renaissance in the sciences, social studies, humanities, and arts in the lower years of elementary education. In fact, it will be recalled, we found a paucity of any of these.

We know that it is exceedingly difficult to change human behavior, even when the individual is young and moderately malleable. But changing the behavior patterns of adults is a task of formidable dimensions, especially when present patterns have been carefully taught through a long, structured system of schooling and are endorsed and protected by that system. It is unreasonable to believe that these patterns will be changed by attending lectures, participating in brief orientation sessions, reading manuals, or even attending a course where the instructor talks about instead of demonstrates new procedures. And yet, these are the accepted approaches to re-educating teachers. It is as though we do not expect anything to happen anyway and so we just go through the established rituals.

The ambitious strategy of bringing scholars and teachers together in the development of new instructional materials and subsequent follow-up in the classroom had some chance of success. But even this promising approach faced formidable obstacles in the structure of schooling. It is not easy to deal with some of the traditional, parental expectations for what mathematics and science should be, based heavily on their experience with what it has been. Administrators frequently keep a keen eye on these expectations and seek to slow change to a tolerable rate, a rate often slower than would be accepted if channels of communication were cultivated. But perhaps even more significant, many of the assumptions underlying recent efforts at curricular change run smack up against long-established assumptions and procedures built into schooling as virtually a way of life.

Thus, for example, the notion that the most important learnings are fundamental concepts and processes to be developed over several years of inquiry tends to be negated by an emphasis on facts and topics "to be covered" in a semester or a grade. Similarly, a varied approach involving experiments, filmstrips, speculative discussions, and group projects makes demands on teaching which the standard textbook approach often does not. Unfortunately, those involved in curriculum change often are unaware of proposals for change in these structural realms or are initially naïve with respect to the restraints of the system. Understandably, they are not prepared to come to grips with the whole of educational change and may very well feel frustrated or impotent in the face of what appears to be required. Little wonder that they return to more scholarly endeavors or redouble their efforts to produce improved instructional products.

Since the teachers usually are only *exposed* to the ideas, whatever the intended change, and have not yet internalized their full meaning before being on their own with the ideas, it is not surprising that there appears to be a gap between what they think they are doing and what we saw them doing. Chances are, most teachers seeking to teach inductively, to use a range of instructional media, to individualize instruction, to nongrade or team teach, have never seen any of these things done well, let alone participated in them to the point of getting a "feel" for them or of how to proceed on their own. We simply do not have in this country an array of exemplary models displaying alternative modes of schooling, in spite of assumed local control and diversity.

Certain preoccupations with evaluation have discouraged the arduous process of developing such exemplary models.

There is, today, a growing and, on the whole, sound drive toward the evaluation of educational activity, particularly so-called innovations. Unfortunately, most of it is mired, still, in the mud of standardized, norm-based achievement tests. Consequently, with the first blush of change comes the charge to measure it — usually in terms of the pupil behaviors conventionally sought in school. Three shortcomings frequently characterize the process. First, the range of pupil behavior appraised is too limited and does not reflect adequately the full intent of the change. Second, little or no effort is made to determine the nature of the change or, in fact, if any change at all has occurred in the program. As a result, evaluation sometimes has produced recommendations for the abolition of an innovation when, in fact, none was in existence. Third, summative evaluation often is attempted prematurely, with the result that negative judgment is passed before the new venture has had time to mature.

We have made too few demands on old educational ideas and practices, meanwhile discouraging or even killing new ideas by premature judgment. It is clear that American schooling desperately needs new approaches to old problems, that change is exceedingly difficult, that formative must precede summative evaluation, and that innovations are fragile. Instead of putting the new to the test of fire, we should be fostering it with tender, loving care.

## The Reconstruction Process

Analysis indicates three critical entry points in seeking to close the gap between the observed condition of our schools and where we would want them to be. The first of these pertains to the initial pedagogical skills developed in future teachers. The second is the updating of these skills on the job. And the third is the continuous reconstruction of schooling to meet the changing conditions of communities and of society in general.

Regarding the first, our findings reveal that persons preparing to teach simply do not acquire an adequate range of instructional activities and techniques for stimulating and challenging the full range of interest and abilities represented in a class of energetic, inquiring children. What teachers do in both the regular program of instruction and in supplementary, enrichment teaching tend toward sameness and to be tied closely to textbooks and workbooks. Traditionally, teacher preparation has provided an abbreviated introduction to some historical and philosophical aspects of education and schooling. In recent years, psychological conditions of human development, general principles of learning, and data on such matters as individual differences among learners have come more to the fore. However, specific procedural considerations of what approach to use in basic instruction or of how to proceed with pupils individually and in groups have not acquired high status in teacher education programs. Teachers, in the main, lack the pedagogical skills required to induce fully effective learning.

There is no point in continuing to tinker with teacher education programs. They must be revamped from top to bottom. In most colleges and universities, persons preparing to teach juggle a few courses in education with courses in their major fields of preparation. They often appear to be motivated more toward acquiring a degree than to developing the skills, aptitudes, and attitudes requisite to a teaching career. This condition will be corrected only when colleges in general and colleges of education in particular fully accept and provide for the fact that teaching is a challenging, difficult role requiring not merely a good general education, but both a commitment and a repertoire of professional competencies. We must approach the education of teachers in the same serious vein we approach the preparation of dentists, lawyers, and physicians. This calls for a fundamentally different and more serious approach to teacher education than has characterized past efforts.

To begin with, the future teacher must be called upon to make a full-time commitment at the time he commences his preparation and must be selected for, not merely admitted to, the teacher education program. Attainment of an arts or sciences degree no longer should be the paramount objective; acquisition of the knowledge, skills, and attitudes of teaching must come to the forefront. The future teacher may very well continue to pursue mathematics, or history, or English but, after deciding to become a teacher, he must pursue these subjects no longer only as a student but also as a future teacher of them. Next, at the outset of this commitment, the future teacher must become involved in the teaching of young people in some responsible way — not as an observer, but as an active participant. This means that he joins a team of adults as one of several persons charged with responsibility for educating a group of children. Whatever the other reasons for endorsing team teaching may be, one good reason is teacher education. Only in a team-teaching situation can a neophyte teacher be involved as an authentic junior colleague, charged with genuine responsibility for children's learning. Such responsible involvement must occur at the outset of a teacher education program and be sustained throughout, from the limited participation of an aide through the increased participation and responsibility of being an intern and, ultimately, a resident teacher.

But such participation does not guarantee the acquisition of pedagogical skills of designing pupil learning, intervening productively in that learning, and evaluating programs. We recommend at least two ingredients for the development of these pedagogical skills. First, critiques of lessons should be an integral part of every teacher education program. That is, each week, a neophyte teacher teaches under the observation of members of the staff, with fellow neophytes in attendance.

Following the teaching performance, a critique occurs, during which what the young teacher did is analyzed, alternatives are proposed, and suggestions are offered. Interestingly, the conduct of such critiques in a school almost invariably is accompanied by increasing participation on the part of other members of the staff. Analyzing the performance of the student teacher is a non-threatening way for experienced teachers to be introduced to modern pedagogical theories and techniques.

The second ingredient for developing pedagogical skills is a mix of academic and clinical personnel on the teacher education staff of the college. The usual faculty of a teacher preparation institution may not be well-prepared for teaching the finer points of pedagogy; they may have been away from the teaching of young people for too long a period of time, and they may not have been exemplary teachers in any case. Their ongoing experience is now with adults, not with children in classrooms. Consequently, these faculty members must be joined by practitioners of a high order — persons who have integrated appropriate theory with the practical, pedagogical implications of that theory. These are the persons James B. Conant had in mind when he recommended the appointment of clinical professors.[3] For the development of pedagogy in the beginning teacher, then, we recommend a mix of clinical and academic professors, persons who know how and who can and do teach young people, on one hand, and persons who can develop and explain the rationales for practice, on the other.

Unfortunately, current teacher preparation occurs in an atmosphere of survival. Future teachers are taught to adjust to and survive in schools which we believe to be inadequate to present-day demands. We recommend that future teachers be prepared, as team members, in school centers committed to the reconstruction of schooling. However, this rhetoric simply does not convey the magnitude and complexity of the task. For the schools that are geared to maintaining the *status quo* and administrators who maintain the system and do not question or challenge it, we propose, by contrast, that at least some schools be designated agents of change, schools in which the norm is change rather than stability.

Clearly, such a charge calls for decentralizing much authority for educational decision-making to the local school under the leadership of principal and teachers in collaboration with children and parents. In effect, we are saying that the same principles of individualization which should guide instruction in the classroom must guide reconstruction of the local school. Each school must be granted freedom far in excess of what prevails now to pursue its destiny in the light of local needs and significant data — these data being primarily the characteristics of the students and their conditions of daily life. Decades ago, the American school, located in small hamlets and towns across this country, enrolled all the children of all the people in a heterogeneous mix. This is no longer the case. There are ghettos, barrios, and silk-stocking districts, each with its own set of conditions and needs. Providing for them differentially in the schools does not mean condoning the differences, nor does it mean maintaining them in perpetuity. Rather, differentiated education for different pupil populations may very well mean the difference between maintaining the *status quo* at a level of dire inequality and opening the doors to human opportunity.

Our study reveals sharply that almost all of the schools we observed pursued a course of bland uniformity regardless of pupil population and school setting. It is our belief that each school faculty should be identifying its most critical problems, engaging in sustained dialogue regarding alternative courses of action, taking action on one or more of these alternatives, and periodically appraising the results. But only 6 percent of the schools we visited came close to following such a course. The others were following built-in prescriptions of surprising uniformity at a time when local diversity and individuality are desperately needed.

The single school, we believe, with its principal, teachers, children, and parents, is the largest organic unit for educational change.[4] All the rest is superstructure, suited at best for communicating exemplary practices and providing a central pool of materials, personnel, and support to enhance the effort of each school to become relevant and dynamic. It follows that more of the resources of school systems must be allocated for the discretionary use of individual school faculties, that in-service education must be school-centered, that new personnel must be selected by the faculties of local schools, that priorities must be a matter for each school to decide, and that principals must be prepared to exercise leadership with their staffs and communities. We commend to the attention of school boards the practice of English Infant Schools in which instructional funds, although pitifully small, are spent by the staff of each school in the light of pupil needs and interests. In this regard, also, we commend the freedom of Infant School headmistresses, working with their teachers, to determine the character of their school in the light of circumstances surrounding it. Principals and teachers in our schools feel impotent in the face of pressing problems of schooling. They must be rejuvenated by being given real authority and then held accountable for what they do with increased freedom and power. And, within this context of local school responsibility and authority, the teachers of tomorrow must be prepared.

Many teachers in the 67 schools we visited were busily engaged in a wide variety of in-service education activities. And yet, it appeared that their pedagogy was not being updated; nor were the problems which they perceived their schools to have being remedied. With respect to these deficiencies, we make two recommendations. First, teachers must be held accountable for acquiring the new skills they need *within a structure that provides and pays for such opportunity*. Just a little contemplation reveals that, in this country, schooling is the largest industry that does not provide for the systematic updating of its personnel at the cost of the enterprise. Teachers, more than most people, take evening and summer courses, at their own expense — but not always to improve their competence as teachers. A significant proportion — far exceeding

*109*

the demand — is preparing to get out of the classroom through preparing for the principalship. Many have only an advanced degree in mind and look forward to the increased salary benefits to be realized on achieving it.

It is past time to set a professional floor for the preparation of teachers. Teachers should be apprenticed for a longer period of time: as aides, interns, and resident teachers, with stipends from the beginning and with a combination of academic and clinical preparation throughout. On completion of such a program, they should be awarded a professional degree — the master of arts in teaching would be appropriate — and it should be assumed that this is the terminal degree for teaching in the same way that the M.D. is a terminal degree for most branches of medicine. From this point on, the enterprise of schooling should provide for in-service updating designed to keep the teacher abreast of modern developments in his field. This can be done best, we think, by employing teachers on a twelve-month basis (with a month of vacation) and by providing, during the year, whatever additional training appears necessary and desirable. The practicing teacher might be expected, then, to teach nine or ten months of the year and to participate for a month or two, not necessarily in a single block of time, in retraining provided and paid for by the school system. Only in this way, we think, will teachers be able to keep up with advances in both subject matter and pedagogy.

Finally, our exploration revealed that teachers simply are not exposed to exemplary models of schools or pedagogy. They seek to nongrade, team teach, and individualize instruction while possessing only the vaguest insights into the nature and actual conduct of such practices. Preoccupied with managing a class all day, teachers have little opportunity to observe alternative procedures. Occasionally, thanks to the grants of foundations and of the federal government, selected individuals and groups are encouraged to observe elsewhere, but such opportunities are the exception rather than the rule and, given the present paucity of exemplary models, even generous provisions for such inter-school visitation would not yield spectacular results in the form of dramatically changed educational practices. Evidence reveals models worth emulating are in short supply; they will continue to be in short supply, we are convinced, until local schools are given both the authority and the responsibility for developing educational programs designed to cope with their unique problems.

## A Strategy for Change

We have said that no single innovation is adequate for the necessary task of reconstructing the schools—the thousands of schools we have, not merely the "free" schools created outside the system. We doubt that any innovation possesses this inherent power; and, if one did, the study reported here suggests that it would become impotent on its way to and through school and classroom door.

The preceding material points to the need for a comprehensive approach, simultaneously encompassing several critical elements of a change process. A five-year study of educational change which parallels the study reported here has sought both to test a general strategy and to gain insights into the dynamics of schools, individually and collectively, endeavoring to improve their functioning. The strategy was implemented and refined in a creation named the League of Cooperating Schools; the eighteen schools in this consortium, in turn, served as the laboratory for studying the processes.[6] Both studies confirm the importance of several critical elements to be accounted for in a strategy for change having some chance to succeed in the face of formidable obstacles. We have argued for most of these elements on preceding pages. Now let us see how they might be put together in a functioning system.

First, the single school is the organic unit for change. This is in preference to the total school district, on one hand, and the individual teacher, on the other. Both of these are important, of course, but both have been foci for change efforts in the past and the record is unimpressive. The district tends to become overly bureaucratized, stifling the initiative of local schools; and the in-service education of individual teachers when not based on the demands of daily teaching seems not to bring fundamental change into the school. Focus on the school unit suggests a new role for the district office characterized by the question, "How do we help each school improve itself?" rather than, "What do we do to make this a good school district?" The differences in implication between these questions are more than symbolic. Likewise, focus on the school suggests that teachers look to improvement of the total environment and each of its parts rather than only to self-improvement activities having little relationship to school problems.

When one begins to think of the school as an organism in this way, one can begin to think, also, of the healthy functioning of that organism. What should be its relationship to the immediate community? To the central office? To other schools? What is healthy internal functioning? In our League study, we defined health for the faculty group as a process of DDAE—dialogue, decision-making, action, and evaluation. The quality of the decision-making process, as both guided and judged by a rigorous set of criteria covering these four sub-processes (DDAE) developed by teacher and principals, is a strong indication, we think, of the school's ability to change—to consider new possibilities and to act on them in creative ways. A degree of decentralization of decision-making to the local school, of a magnitude tried in only a few small communities, is called for.

Second, the single school is linked with other schools in a new social system characterized by certain elements as described below. While the single school is the locus for change in the new social system, comprising the League, it is not sufficiently powerful, we think, to overcome the generally conservative contingencies of the larger educational enterprise. A linkage with other schools in a consortium committed to self-improvement provides a reinforcing reference group. In our strategy, membership in the League of Cooperating Schools frequently gave schools the support needed to make special requests of the central office and, frequently, to keep going. In time, the League provided a new set of norms, a reward structure, and much of the stimulus for trying new things. The existence and structure of the League described above reinforced processes of DDAE in the individual schools. It became a new social system at first offering alternatives to mere survival in a bureaucratic structure but ultimately becoming sufficiently powerful to modify that structure, with the impact varying from modest to considerable. Principals and teachers seeking to bring about change in their schools were reinforced in their efforts by membership in the League and were able to overcome resistance to change in the school systems of which they were a part. Obviously, establishing cause-and-effect relationships in regard to something so inherently complex is exceedingly difficult. Accompanying research is endeavoring to sort out some of these relationships.

Third, there is a nucleus or hub for the new social system of the League. The hub serves as a center for information, communication, meetings, and the like. We found this to be an exceedingly important part of our total strategy but there are many unanswered questions. Should the hub be identified with some external influence—such as a person, organization, university, etc.—with prestige and recognition, thus legitimatizing whatever changes or innovations are attempted? Can such a hub operate effectively out of a county office, as in the Illinois and California educational structure, where the county school offices have certain service functions assigned to them? Can it be organized effectively by the collaborating schools acting on their own initiative? All of these are possibilities to be tested.

The purposes of the hub range from coordination and training to the dissemination of information and maintenance of communication. Our central offices served as the hub throughout, with personnel from the cooperating schools increasingly taking the initiative in fulfilling all of these purposes. Subsequently, the schools of the League, expanded from 18 to a membership of 25, financed and managed their own hub. Initially, the hub played a major role in training the principals to provide appropriate leadership in their schools and in suggesting ideas for consideration in the schools. Later, however, school personnel showed an increasing desire to learn from each other; a main function of the hub became that of bringing interested parties together. For example, a "classified ad" section of the League newsletter, *Changing Schools*, written by the teachers but edited at the hub, provided a ready means for individuals or whole schools to communicate regarding mutual desires to teach and learn from each other. One faculty group, flushed with success in a project, "advertised" as follows: "Learning how to individualize learning. Interested? Call _____ School at (telephone number)." Another advertised as follows: "Having trouble team teaching? Need help from those who have gone before? Call _____ School at (telephone number)." The hub served to bring together for working seminars those needing and those wanting to give help. There is no question that the hub provided both symbolic and tangible proof that a true collaboration existed.

Also, of great importance, the hub served to screen and give legitimacy to new ideas in such a way that it was easier than it might have been otherwise for the school staffs to select among alternatives. At times, this occurred in very subtle ways which we still are trying to understand.

Fourth, in-service education activities of personnel is indigenous to the school; the activities rise out of the demands of change and daily teaching. Consequently, the support and reward system supported and endorsed by the League strategy operate as reinforcing contingencies for in-service activity designed to improve both the school and personal teaching. In the study reported in this volume, we saw that much—in fact, most—in-service education activities are not of this kind. Rather they tend to take teachers away from the schools and their problems. In-service teacher education is caught up in a host of long-established rituals that are not easily abandoned: school-district sponsored institutes on a miscellaneous array of topics; district-wide curriculum planning projects; and university courses for degrees. Consequently, many of the League teachers and principals found themselves expending energies for these traditional activities (largely because of the reward system), as well as for the activities being reinforced by League members. The combined load proved to be one of our most vexing problems in that these distracting activities tended to take teacher time and energy away from the vital, demanding tasks of improving their own schools.

What is necessary for effective change, we think, is for individual and school needs to be identified through participation in school improvement processes and then met through learning opportunities created specifically for these needs. This is precisely what happened in the League. For example, after examining the possibilities of alternative approaches to teaching and learning, a group of teachers used the newsletter to establish communication with teachers farther along with such processes, ultimately setting up Saturday morning workshops for mutual assistance on problems of individualizing instruction. Sometimes, the hub was able to arrange for consultant help for these self-inspired and arranged activities. It becomes apparent that school systems should give in-service credit to teachers who take such additional hours to deal with tasks so directly related to improving their own schools and teaching.

The support system for more effective in-service education, in the total strategy we recommend, includes more realistic provision for faculty planning time than currently prevails. This takes two forms: time from daily duties; and an extended teaching year. In some states, there are legal provisions for minimum days (the children are released early) or in-service days to facilitate staff planning. But minimum days are insufficient. It is foolhardy to think that tired teachers, in a few meetings each year, can effect truly fundamental reform in curriculum, school organization, or teaching. Some schools get around the problem partially by team teaching arrangements which facilitate the release of staff; by rearranging the school year to provide planning weeks after several weeks of teaching; or by three months of school followed by a month of planning (and, once each year, a month of vacation). We think the ultimate answer lies in employing at least the tenured full-time staff for eleven months each year, with the usual nine of these to be devoted to teaching duties and the other two to redesigning the school program and to personal improvement directly related to school and classroom demands. Individual schools should have a considerable measure of flexibility within certain essential guidelines in determining both school and individual time schedules for the year.

In many ways, what is proposed in an enlarged change strategy eliminates much of the distinction between pre-service and in-service teacher education. The teacher-in-training becomes a beginning teacher, a junior colleague on a school faculty. The role of the university-based teacher training faculty becomes redefined, too, and now works in a team relationship with school personnel. Teacher education and the schools are reconstructed simultaneously.[7]

What we propose for the reconstruction of schooling will be disappointing to many. We offer no panaceas. We offer no gadgets, levers to pull, or buttons to push. The more we delve into this vital business of improving the schools, the more certain we are that there are no easy answers. And the more we look beyond the schools to many who would change them, the more apparent it becomes that the most important principle of all is not getting through to enough people: *For the schools to change, the people in them must change.* Changing people, especially full-grown people, is the most difficult of all human enterprises. When we recognize this, perhaps we will go about the business of improving schools in serious, systematic, and systemic ways that have some chance of success. These ways involve, primarily, changing the expectations and activities of those behind the classroom door.

## Notes

1. See, for example, Leslie A. Hart, *The Classroom Disaster* (New York: Teachers College Press, 1969); Philip W. Jackson, *Life in Classrooms* (New York: Holt, Rinehart and Winston, Inc., 1968); A. Harry Passow, ed., *Reactions to Silberman's "Crisis in the Classroom"* (Worthington, Ohio: Charles A. Jones Publishing Company, 1971).

2. John I. Goodlad, "The Schools Versus Education," *Saturday Review*, April, 19, 1969.

3. The charge of dehumanization in schools, among others, has led to proposals for alternatives to schooling. For a presentation and analysis of some of the issues see Daniel U. Levine and Robert J. Havighurst, eds., *Farewell to Schools???* (Worthington, Ohio: Charles A. Jones Publishing Company, 1971).

4. James B. Conant, *The Education of American Teachers* (New York: McGraw-Hill Book Co., 1963).

5. John I. Goodlad, "The Individual School and Its Principal: Key Setting and Key Person in Educational Leadership," *Educational Leadership* 13 (October, 1955): 2-6.

6. The strategy was implemented, refined, and studied in a consortium of schools set up for the purposes of effecting and understanding educational change. Under the auspices of the Institute for Development of Educational Activities, Inc., an affiliate of the Charles F. Kettering Foundation, eighteen schools were brought together in the League of Cooperating Schools which served as a laboratory for this work. The findings are being prepared for publication as this revised edition goes to press. Early reports on the purposes of this work include Virgil M. Howes, "A Strategy for Research and Change: The League of Cooperating Schools," *Childhood Education* 44 (September, 1967): 68-69; and John

I. Goodlad, "Educational Change: A Strategy for Study and Action," *The National Elementary Principal* XLVIII (January, 1969): 6-13.

7. John I. Goodlad, "The Reconstruction of Teacher Education," *Teachers College Record* 72 (September, 1970): 61-72.

# Appendix

# Instrument for Study
# of Childhood Schooling

We present here a somewhat revised version of the instrument used in gathering the data analyzed on preceding pages. We have profited much from the suggestions of our students who have used it for research and other purposes. Many requests coming to us from educators in this country and abroad impressed upon us the importance of adding both sections of it to this edition of *Looking Behind the Classroom Door*.

Many courses in education require observation of classes on the part of students. We think the instrument is particularly useful for such a purpose, provided it is used for penetrating, anecdotal-type recording of what goes on in schools and not merely for casual observation. We urge instructors not to send out their students without careful, preliminary discussion and training.

The instrument presented on the following pages is a guide to gathering information on schools. It points to a greater array of data than can be collected easily by a single observer/interviewer. Consequently, the college or university instructor seeking to use the guide with teacher education classes is urged to divide the task of gathering data among several persons. These can then come together following the observation to provide a comprehensive picture of school and classroom. Even if time to fill out the complete instrument is not available, we think the various categories and sub-categories might be useful in alerting students to the complex array of concerns making up a school. There is a tendency on the part of most people to view schools in unrealistic, simplistic terms.

We have included substantial lists of readings for major categories because we assume that college and university instructors want their students to think seriously about and understand what goes on in schools and to consider viable alternatives. We think that an entire course or seminar might be organized around observation in schools and classrooms, using the instrument and readings for guidance and for organizing discussions, preparing papers and reports. It must be remembered that subsequent pages present a guide to anecdotal recording. The instrument is not a checklist. Its use should result in a carefully-ordered paper describing the daily conduct of schools and classrooms.

At the beginning of our study, we searched the literature for procedures and instruments for use in observing the school and classroom as entities. We found no appropriate framework which was broad enough for our interests. Instruments for various dimensions within schooling existed. Some of these had been very carefully designed and standardized, but they were too specific and too in-depth in a limited number of areas for the purposes of present study. As a result of our search, we decided that it was necessary to devise our own instrument for assessing school and classroom.

The instrument has not been standardized in any formal way but is the result of several field studies, much reading, and analyses of schools and classrooms. Responses to the items in the instrument will require collecting information from interviews with principals and teachers as well as from direct observation. Some of the components are easily quantified and assessed; others are far more difficult to assess and quantify. The assessments of skillful and knowledgeable observers on these dimensions should provide important data for use in attempting to study and improve the process of schooling.

The total instrument consists of two parts: one for studying a school and one for studying a classroom. The parts should be modified to meet the needs of each person using them and could be supplemented by standardized instruments developed to study given aspects in greater depth. We offer what follows not as *the* way to study a school and classroom, but as *one* way to observe, record, and analyze comprehensively their complexities.

Our experience tells us that this guide to the observation of school and classroom practices is exceedingly useful for research and that it can be adapted readily for use in most countries. Since completing the study reported here, we have become intrigued with the potentiality of the instrument, accompanied by readings, as a framework for organizing teacher education classes, both pre-service and in-service. We find that even experienced teachers are unaccustomed to observing the classes of others and, in fact, are helped by this observation guide. Armed with such a guide, they come to think about schooling with the perspective of "really seeing."

We thank our students who have helped not only to revise both sections but also to extend our awareness of their potential usefulness. We thank, especially, Lillian K. Drag for her usual high level of competence in assisting us with the suggestions for reading.

# Part One: School Information

Observer_____ Date_____
School_____ District_____
City_____ State_____
Name and position of person giving information _____

How long interviewed _____
Conditions of interview _____

    I. Physical Properties of School (*See* page 136 for References)

      A. Number of Personnel

        1. Number of pupils in school

        2. Number of teachers

        3. Pupil-teacher ratio

        4. Approximate number of pupils in individual classes

        5. Age range of pupils

        6. Number of specialists

            Fulltime                 Parttime

      B. School Construction
        1. Type (Descriptive statement of building materials used)

        2. Arrangement of rooms (Statement of physical arrangement)

        3. Number of floors in facilities

        4. Design (Statement of utilization of space)

        5. Age of plant

        6. Safety of buildings

C. Other Physical Facilities Available

   1. On school grounds

   2. In community

D. Attractiveness of Buildings and Grounds

II. Organization of School (*See* page 136 for References)

   A. Indicate whether total school has the same organizational pattern or what portions of school are in any given organizational pattern

   B. Vertical Organization (Statement of how students are organized to progress through long blocks of time such as semesters or years)

   C. Horizontal Organization (Statement of how students are organized for the school day)

III. Institutional Curriculum (*See* page 137 for References)

   A. Goals (Statement of what students are expected to achieve while attending school)

      1. Stated or inferred objectives of school

      2. How and by whom developed

      3. Extent to which implemented in classrooms

   B. Evaluation (Statement of how student progress is determined)

      1. Means of evaluation for school

      2. Purposes of evaluation for school

   C. General Curriculum Design (Statement regarding how the expected student achievements are organized for learning)

   D. Sources of Institutional Curriculum

   E. Flexibility for Teachers in Implementation   .

   F. Uniqueness of Institutional Curriculum

G. Problems in Institutional Curriculum

H. Degree of Balance in Curriculum (Degree of emphasis among curriculum areas)

IV. School Personnel (*See* page 138 for References)

A. Type, Number, and Amount of Professional Preparation and Experience

| Position | Number | Amount of professional preparation | Professional experience |
|---|---|---|---|
| 1. Principal | | | |
| 2. Vice Principals | | | |
| 3. Department heads Counselors Team leaders | | | |
| 4. Consultants (specify type) | | | |
| 5. Specialists (specify type) | | | |
| 6. Teachers | | | |
| 7. Assistant teachers | | | |
| 8. Teacher aides | | | |
| 9. Volunteers | | | |
| 10. Custodians | | | |
| 11. Secretaries | | | |
| 12. Cafeteria workers | | | |
| 13. Others (specify) | | | |

B. Role of Specialists and Consultants in the Program (Based on only professionally trained, available personnel)

V. Resources (*See* page 140 for References)

A. Community Resources

1. Regularly used

2. Occasionally used

B. School Resources

1. Library—curriculum center

Resources                   Extent of use

                        How used (by whom,
               Type    how often, how freely)

2. Laboratories

3. Audiovisual equipment

4. Gymnasium— playgrounds

5. Outdoor equipment

VI. Special Provisions of School (Statement regarding what this school provides that many other schools might not)

A. Special Program Emphases

B. Special Sources of Funds

                    Source        How used

C. Special Classes

D. Special Resources Available and Utilized

VII. Record Keeping and Reporting (*See* page 141 for References)

A.    Records        Types        Uses made of records

B.  Reports

    Group (to which
        report goes)    Type of report    Frequency reported

VIII. Significant Problems of School and Attempts to Solve Them (*See* page 142 for References)

    A.  Listing of Problems and Methods of Solution

        Problem        Method of solution

IX. Uniqueness of School (*See* page 142 for References)

    A.  Uniqueness

X. General Impressional Observations (*See* page 142 for References)

    A.  Impressions, including assessment of cultural and emotional climate of school

# Part Two: Classroom Information

Observer_____ Date_____
Teacher_____ School_____
Ages or grade levels _____ Total time in classroom_____
How long interview lasted_____ Conditions of interview_____
Was behavior and program considered to be typical
   by teacher_____ by observer_____
General schedule of teacher _____

I. Physical Properties of Classroom (*See* page 143 for References)

   A. Number of Pupils

   B. Number of Teachers

   C. Pupil-Teacher Ratio (Include only professionally trained persons)

   D. Age Range of Pupils

   E. Size and Arrangement of Classroom

   F. Flexibility of Space

   G. Auxiliary Facilities Available to Classroom

   H. Safety of Classroom

   I. Availability and Use of Space by Students

   J. Physical Attractiveness of Classroom

II. Classroom Organization (*See* page 143 for References)

   A. Type of Vertical Organization (Statement of how students are organized for progression through long blocks of time—semester or year)

*129*

B. Type of Horizontal Organization (Statement of how students are organized for short periods of time—school day)

C. Types of Groups in Evidence, Flexibility, Composition, and Purpose of Groups

D. Degree of Organization in the Program

E. General Scheme of Daily Program

F. General Scheme of Weekly or Longer Range Program

III. Instructional Curriculum (*See* page 144 for References)

A. Objectives

1. Stated or inferred objectives of activities observed

2. Source(s) of objectives

3. Means of evaluation

a. teacher observation

b. standardized educational tests of progress (specify)

c. psychological and medical tests (specify)

d. physical measurements (specify)

e. other (specify)

4. Purposes of evaluation

B. Sources of Total Instructional Curriculum

C. Flexibility Allowed Teacher in Implementing Above Sources in Classroom

D. Teacher Assessment of Curriculum

E. Balance in Curricular Areas (Degree of emphasis among curricular areas)

F. Description and Assessment of Major Organizing Centers (How stimuli are presented to students so that learning can occur)

IV. Classroom Personnel (*See* page 145 for References)

    A. Teacher

        1. Amount of professional preparation

        2. Professional experience: Years      Grades

        3. Perceived role of teacher by teachers

        4. Actual role of teacher in operation

        5. Teacher perception of groups (Functions of groups and how they operate)

        6. Availability and use of sources for professional growth

        7. Degree to which teacher engages in self-evaluation

    B. Specialists or Consultants

        1. Number, type, and when used in program

            Number          Type          When used

        2. Role in classroom program

    C. Auxiliary Personnel

        1. Number, type, when used, general level of education, and experience of each

            Number        Type        When used
            Level of education        Experience

        2. Role in classroom program

    D. Students

        1. Range of socioeconomic background

        2. Ethnic-racial backgrounds in group

        3. Types of students in groups

        4. Role in planning and implementing program and evaluating growth

V. Materials and Equipment in Evidence (*See* page 145 for References)

Place checkmark in front of all those materials and equipment actually in use in the classroom.

A. Books

_____ 1. Number and range of library books

_____ 2. Number and range of textbooks

_____ 3. Number and range of programmed materials

_____ 4. Number and range of reference materials

B. Other Printed Materials

_____ 1. Number and range of maps

_____ 2. Number and range of pamphlets and other such documents

_____ 3. Number and range of magazines

_____ 4. Other (specify)

C. Audiovisual Materials

_____ 1. Number and use of bulletin boards

_____ 2. General availability and frequency of use of films

_____ filmstrips

_____ overhead projectors

_____ study prints

_____ tape recorders

_____ record players

_____ other (specify)

D. Availability and Use of Music Materials

E. Availability and Use of Science Materials

F. Availability and Use of Math Materials

G. Availability and Use of Art Materials

H. Availability and Use of Other Materials (specify)

VI. Instruction (*See* page 146 for References)

A. Modes Used

B. Role of Teacher(s)

C. Role of Learner(s)

D. Domain(s) of Instruction

1. Cognitive

2. Affective

3. Psychomotor

4. Performance

E. Level or Range of Instruction

F. Use of Learning Theory

1. Motivation

2. Reinforcement

3. Knowledge of results

4. Degree and type of learner involvement in planning, implementing, and evaluating program

5. Opportunity for transfer

G. Evaluation of Instruction

Frequency                    Means

H. Degree and Success of Individualization in Various Areas of Program

VII. Classroom Climate and Interaction Patterns (*See* page 146 for References)

A. Degree of Pupil-to-Pupil Patterns

B. Quality of Pupil-to-Pupil Interaction

C. Degree of Pupil-to-Teacher Interaction

D. Quality of Pupil-to-Teacher Interaction

E. Degree of Teacher-to-Pupil Interaction

F. Quality of Teacher-to-Pupil Interaction

G. Mood and Morale of Pupils

H. Mood and Morale of Teachers

I. Mood and Morale of Teacher Aides

J. Mode, Frequency, and Quality of Teacher Reinforcement (Methods of discipline)

K. General Involvement of Pupils

L. General Involvement of Teachers

M. General Involvement of Other Personnel

    1. Aides

    2. Specialists

    3. Consultants

    4. Volunteers

N. Freedom within Program

    1. Of teachers

    2. Of students

VIII. Significant Problems of Classroom and Attempts to Solve Them (*See* page 147 for References)

Keep separate problems identified by observer and those identified by teacher.

A. Observer-Noted Problems      Method of Solution

B. Teacher-Noted Problems      Methods of Solution

# References

Part One: School Information

I. References for Physical Properties of School (*See* page 124)

Abramson, Paul. *Schools for Early Childhood.* A Report from Educational Facilities Laboratories. New York: Educational Facilities Laboratories, 1970.

Allen, Lady of Hurtwood. *Planning for Play.* Cambridge, Mass.: The M.I.T. Press, 1968.

American Association of School Administrators. *Open Space Schools.* Washington, D. C.: The Association, 1971.

Anderson, Robert H. "The School as an Organic Teaching Aid." In *The Curriculum: Retrospect and Prospect,* 70th Yearbook, Part I. National Society for the Study of Education. Chicago: University of Chicago Press, 1971, pp. 271-306.

Clinchy, Evans. *Joint Occupancy: Profiles of Significant Schools.* A Report from Educational Facilities Laboratories. New York: Educational Facilities Laboratory, 1970.

Gross, Ronald, and Murphy, Judith. *Educational Change and Architectural Consequences: A Report on Facilities for Individualized Instruction.* New York: Educational Facilities Laboratories, 1968.

Metropolitan Toronto School Board. *Educational Specifications and User Requirements for Elementary (K-6) Schools.* Toronto, Canada: Ryerson Press, 1968.

*The Open Plan School.* Report of a National Seminar. Co-sponsored by Educational Facilities Laboratories and /I/D/E/A/. Dayton, Ohio: Institute for Development of Educational Activities, Inc., 1970.

Toffler, Alvin, ed. *The Schoolhouse in the City.* New York: Praeger Publishers, 1968.

II. References for Organization of School (*See* page 125)

Alexander, William M. et al. *The Emergent Middle School.* New York: Holt, Rinehart & Winston, 1968.

Anderson, Robert H. *Teaching in a World of Change.* New York: Harcourt, Brace & World, 1966.

Franklin, Marian P., ed. *School Organization: Theory and Practice.* Chicago: Rand McNally & Co., 1969.

Goodlad, John I. "Toward Improved School Organization." *Planning and Organizing for Teaching.* Washington, D. C.: NEA Project on the Instructional Program of the Public Schools, 1963, pp. 52-92.

Goodlad, John I., and Anderson, Robert H. *The Nongraded Elementary School.* Rev. ed. New York: Harcourt, Brace & World, 1963.

Heathers, Glen. "School Organization." In *The Changing American School.* 65th Yearbook, Part II. National Society for the Study of Education. Chicago: University of Chicago Press, 1966, pp. 110-34.

Hillson, Maurie, and Bongo, Joseph. *Continuous Progress Education.* Palo Alto, Calif.: Science Research Associates, 1971.

Hillson, Maurie, and Hyman, Ronald T. eds. *Change and Innovation in Elementary and Secondary Organizations.* 2nd ed. New York: Holt, Rinehart & Winston, 1971.

Overly, Donald E.; Kinghorn, Jon Rye; Preston, Richard L. *The Middle School: Humanizing Education for Youth.* Worthington, Ohio: Charles A. Jones Publishing, 1971.

*Multi-Age Grouping: Enriching the Learning Environment.* Washington, D. C.: NEA Department of Elementary-Kindergarten-Nursery Education, 1968.

Shaplin, Judson T., and Olds, Henry F., Jr., eds. *Team Teaching.* New York: Harper & Row, 1964.

III. References for Institutional Curriculum (*See* page 125)

Association for Supervision and Curriculum Development. *Balance in the Curriculum.* 1961 Yearbook. Washington, D. C.: The Association, 1961.

Bloom, Benjamin S. et al. *Handbook on Formative and Summative Evaluation of Student Learning.* New York: McGraw-Hill Book Company, Inc., 1971.

Burns, Richard W., and Brooks, Gary D., eds. *Curriculum Design in a Changing Society.* Englewood Cliffs, N. J.: Educational Technology Publications, 1970.

Frymier, Jack R., and Hawn, Horace C. *Curriculum Improvement for Better Schools.* Worthington, Ohio: Charles A. Jones Publishing, 1970.

Goodlad, John I. "Toward Improved Curriculum Organization." *Planning and Organizing for Teaching.* Washington, D. C.: NEA Project on the Instructional Program of the Public Schools, 1963, pp. 24-51.

Goodlad, John I., with Richter, Maurice N., Jr. *The Development of a Conceptual System for Dealing with Problems of Curriculum and Instruction.* Report of an inquiry supported by the Cooperative Research Program, U. S. Department of Health, Education, and Welfare. Los Angeles: University of California and /I/D/E/A/, 1966.

Hauenstein, Dean A. *Curriculum Planning for Behavioral Development.* Worthington, Ohio: Charles A. Jones Publishing, 1972.

Herrick, Virgil E. *Strategies of Curriculum Development.* Compiled and edited by James B. Macdonald, Dan W. Anderson, and Frank B. May. Columbus, Ohio: Charles E. Merrill Books, 1965.

Hoepfner, Ralph; Bradley, P. A.; Klein, S. P.; and M. Alkin. *Elementary School Evaluation Kit: Needs Assessment.* Los Angeles: Center for the Study of Evaluation, University of California, 1971.

Joyce, Bruce R. *Alternative Models of Elementary Education.* Waltham, Mass.: Blaisdell Publishing, 1969.

National Society for the Study of Education. *The Curriculum: Retrospect and Prospect.* 70th Yearbook. Part I. Robert M. McClure, ed. Chicago: University of Chicago Press, 1971.

NEA Center for the Study of Instruction. *Rational Planning in Curriculum and Instruction.* Washington, D. C.: The Center, 1967.

Short, Edmund C., and Marconnit, George D. eds. *Contemporary Thought on Public School Curriculum.* Dubuque, Iowa: William C. Brown, Publishers, 1968.

Weinstein, Gerald, and Fantini, Mario D., eds. *Toward Humanistic Education: A Curriculum of Affect.* New York: Praeger Publishers, 1970.

IV. References for School Personnel (*See* page 126)

Allen, Dwight W. "A Differentiated Staff: Putting Teaching Talent to Work." *NEA Occasional Paper.* Washington, D. C.: NEA National Commission on Teacher Education and Professional Standards, 1967.

Allen, Paul M.; Barnes, William D.; Roberson, E. Wayne; and Reece, Jerald L. *Teacher Self-Appraisal: A Way of Looking Over Your Own Shoulder.* Worthington, Ohio: Charles A. Jones Publishing, 1970.

Bennett, William S., Jr., and Falk, R. Frank. *New Careers and Urban Schools.* New York: Holt, Rinehart & Winston, 1970.

Bowman, Gerda W., and Klopf, Gordon J. *New Careers and Roles in the American Schools.* New York: Bank Street College of Education, 1968.

Crenshaw, Joseph W. et al. *Flexible Staff Organization Study.* Interim Report. Tallahassee, Fla.: Florida State Department of Education, Division of Curriculum and Instruction, 1969.

*Differentiated Staffing: Giving Teaching a Chance to Improve Learning.* Temple City, Calif.: Temple City Unified School District, 1969.

Doll, Ronald C. *Leadership to Improve Schools.* Worthington, Ohio: Charles A. Jones Publishing, 1972.

*Differentiated Staffing in Schools.* Education U. S. A. Special Report. Washington, D. C.: National Schools Public Relations Association, 1970.

Frazier, Alexander, ed. *The New Elementary School.* Washington, D. C.: Association for Supervision and Curriculum Development, 1968.

Goodlad, John I. "Toward Improved Personnel Resources, Time, and Space Organization." In *Planning and Organizing for Teaching.* Washington, D. C.: NEA Project on the Instructional Program of the Public Schools, 1963, pp. 119-38.

Joyce, Bruce R. *The Teacher and His Staff: Man, Media and Machines.* Washington, D. C.: NEA National Commission on Teacher Education and Professional Standards, 1967.

Kimbrough, Ralph B. *Administering Elementary Schools: Concepts and Practices.* New York: Macmillan Co., 1968.

Lewis, James, Jr. *Differentiating the Teaching Staff.* West Nyack, N. Y.: Parker Publishing, 1971.

Melaragno, Ralph S., and Newmark, Gerald. *Tutorial Community Project.* Santa Monica, Calif.: System Development Corporation, 1970.

Shane, June Grant; Shane, Harold G.; Gibson, Robert L.; and Munger, Paul F. *Guiding Human Development: The Counselor and the*

*Teacher in the Elementary School.* Worthington, Ohio: Charles A. Jones Publishing, 1971.

V. References for Resources (*See* page 127)

American Association of School Administrators. *Instructional Technology and the School Administrator.* Washington, D. C.: The Association, 1970.

American Library Association and National Education Association. *Standards for School Media Programs.* Chicago, Ill.: American Library Association; Washington, D. C.: NEA, 1969.

Association for Childhood Education International. *Equipment and Supplies.* Washington, D. C.: The Association, 1968.

———. *Learning Centers: Children on Their Own.* Washington, D. C.: The Association, 1970.

Goodlad, John I. "Toward Improved Personnel Resources, Time, and Space Organization." *Planning and Organizing for Teaching.* Washington, D. C.: NEA Project on the Instructional Program of the Public Schools, 1963, pp. 119-38.

Joyce, Bruce R. *The Teacher and His Staff: Man, Media and Machines.* Washington, D. C.: NEA, 1967.

Pearson, Neville P., and Butler, Lucius. *Instructional Materials Centers: Selected Readings.* Minneapolis, Minn.: Burgess Publishing Co., 1969.

Pula, Fred John, and Goff, Robert J. *Technology in Education: Challenge and Change.* Worthington, Ohio: Charles A. Jones Publishing, 1972.

*Selecting Instructional Materials for Purchase: Procedural Guidelines.* Joint Committee of NEA and the Association of American Publishers. Washington, D. C.: NEA, 1971.

Umans, Shelley. *The Management of Education.* Garden City, N. Y.: Doubleday & Co., 1970.

U. S. Congress. House Committee on Education and Labor. *To Improve Learning.* A Report to the President and the Congress by the Commission on Instructional Technology. Washington, D. C.: U.S.G.P.O., March 1970.

U. S. Office of Education. *Descriptive Case Studies of Nine Elementary School Media Centers in Three Inner Cities.* Washington, D. C.: U.S.G.P.O., 1969.

Weisgerber, Robert A., ed. *Instructional Process and Media Innovation.* Chicago: Rand McNally & Co., 1968.

Wiman, Raymond V. *Instructional Materials.* Worthington, Ohio: Charles A. Jones Publishing, 1972.

*See also* page 136 for References listed for Part One: School Information, I. Physical Properties of School

VII. References for Record Keeping and Reporting (*See* page 127)

Ahmann, J. Stanley, and Glock, Marvin D. *Evaluating Pupil Growth.* Boston: Allyn and Bacon, 1967.

Goodlad, John I., and Anderson, Robert H. *The Nongraded Elementary School.* Rev. ed. New York: Harcourt, Brace & World, Inc., 1963, chapter 6.

Hillson, Maurie, and Bongo, Joseph. *Continuous Progress Education.* Palo Alto, Calif.: Science Research Associates, 1971, chapter 6.

Lambert, Nadine M. et al. *The Stress of School Project: Anecdotal Processing to Promote the Learning Experience.* (USPHS, NIH Grants MH 14, 605-01 and 02). Berkeley, Calif.: University of California, Stress of School Project, 1970.

NEA Research Division. *Marking and Reporting Pupil Progress.* Research Summary 1970-SI. Washington, D. C.: The Association, 1970.

Russell Sage Foundation. *Guidelines for the Collection, Maintenance, and Dissemination of Pupil Records.* Report of a Conference on the Ethical and Legal Aspects of School Record Keeping. Hartford, Conn.: Russell Sage Foundation, 1970.

Sawin, Enoch, I. *Evaluation and the Work of the Teacher.* Belmont, Calif.: Wadsworth Publishing Co., 1969, chapter 13.

*A Teacher's Guide to Retrieval and Reporting Practices* (ESEA Title III Project). Salt Lake City: Continuous Progress Education, 1969.

Thomas, R. Murray. *Judging Student Progress.* 2d ed. New York: David McKay Co., 1960, chapter 14.

Wrinkle, William L. *Improving Marking and Reporting Practices in Elementary and Secondary Schools.* New York: Holt, Rinehart & Winston, 1947.

VIII. References for Significant Problems of School and Attempts to Solve Them (*See* page 128)

Glasser, William. *Schools Without Failure.* New York: Harper & Row, 1969.

Glogau, Lillian, and Fessell, Murray. *The Nongraded Primary School: A Case Study.* West Nyack, N. Y.: Parker Publishing Co., 1967.

Havighurst, Robert J., and Levine, Daniel U., eds. *Farewell to Schools???* Worthington, Ohio: Charles A. Jones Publishing, 1971.

Hoepfner, Ralph; Bradley, P. A.; Klein, S. P.; and Alkin, M. *Elementary School Evaluation Kit: Needs Assessment.* Los Angeles: Center for the Study of Evaluation, University of California, 1971.

Lutz, Frank W., ed. *Toward Improved Urban Education.* Worthington, Ohio: Charles A. Jones Publishing, 1970.

Schmuck, Richard A., and Runkel, Philip J. *Organizational Training for a School Faculty.* Eugene, Oreg.: Center for the Advanced Study of Educational Administration, University of Oregon, 1970.

Watson, Goodwin, ed. *Change in School Systems.* Washington, D. C.: NEA National Training Laboratories, 1967.

IX. References for Uniqueness of School (*See* page 128)

Von Haden, Herbert I. and King, Jean Marie. *Educational Innovator's Guide.* Worthington, Ohio: Charles A. Jones Publishing, 1974.

———. *Innovations in Education: Their Pros and Cons.* Worthington, Ohio: Charles A. Jones Publishing, 1971.

X. References for General Impressional Observations (*See* page 128)

Featherstone, Joseph. *Schools Where Children Learn.* New York: Harper & Row, 1971.

Hart, Leslie A. *The Classroom Disaster.* New York: Teachers College Press, 1969.

Hentoff, Nat. *Our Children Are Dying.* New York: Viking Press, 1966.

Levenson, William B. *The Spiral Pendulum.* Chicago: Rand McNally & Co., 1968.

Mayer, Martin. *The Schools.* New York: Harper & Row, 1961.

Parker, Don H. *Schooling for What?* New York: McGraw-Hill Book Co., 1970.

Passow, A. Harry, ed. *Reactions to Silberman's "Crisis in the Classroom."* Worthington, Ohio: Charles A. Jones Publishing, 1971.

Sarason, Seymour. *The Culture of the School and the Problem of Change.* Boston: Allyn & Bacon, 1971.

Schrag, Peter. *Voices in the Classroom: Public Schools and Public Attitudes.* Boston: Beacon Press, 1965.

Silberman, Charles E. *Crisis in the Classroom: The Remaking of American Education.* New York: Random House, 1970.

Smith, Louis M., and Keith, Pat M. *Anatomy of Educational Innovation: An Organizational Analysis of an Elementary School.* New York: John Wiley, 1971.

Part Two: Classroom Information
    I. References for Physical Properties of Classroom (*See* page 129)

Goodlad, John I. "Toward Improved Personnel Resources, Time, and Space Organization." In *Planning and Organizing for Teaching.* Washington, D. C.: NEA Project on the Instructional Program of the Public Schools, 1963, pp. 119-38.

*The Open Plan School.* Report of a National Seminar co-sponsored by Educational Facilities Laboratories and /I/D/E/A/. Dayton, Ohio: Institute for Development of Educational Activities, Inc. 1970.

*See also* page 136 for References listed for Part One: School Information, I. Physical Properties of School

    II. References for Classroom Organization (*See* page 129)

Association for Childhood Education International. *Learning Centers: Children On Their Own.* Washington, D. C.: The Association, 1970.

Goodlad, John I. "Toward Improved Classroom Organization." In *Planning and Organizing for Teaching.* Washington, D. C.: NEA Project on the Instructional Program of the Public Schools, 1963, pp. 93-118.

Heathers, Glen. "Guidelines for Reorganizing the School and the Classroom." In *Rational Planning in Curriculum and Instruction.* Washington, D. C.: Center for the Study of Instruction, NEA, 1967, pp. 63-86.

Kohl, Herbert R. *The Open Classroom: A Practical Guide to a New Way of Teaching.* New York: New York Review Vintage, 1969.

Morgenstern, Anne, ed. *Grouping in the Elementary School.* New York: Pitman Publishing, 1966.

Thelen, Herbert A. et al. *Classroom Grouping for Teachability.* Chicago: University of Chicago Press, 1967.

Westby-Gibson, Dorothy. *Grouping Students for Improved Instruction.* Englewood Cliffs, N. J.: Prentice-Hall, 1966.

III. References for Instructional Curriculum (*See* page 130)

Association for Supervision and Curriculum Development, NEA *Perceiving, Behaving, Becoming, a New Focus for Education.* 1962 Yearbook. Washington, D. C.: The Association, 1962.

Goodlad, John I. *School, Curriculum, and the Individual.* Waltham, Mass.: Blaisdell Publishing, 1969.

––––––. "The Organizing Center in Curriculum Theory and Practice." *Theory Into Practice* 1 (Feb., 1962): 215-21.

––––––. "The Teacher Selects, Plans, Organizes." *Learning and the Teacher.* 1959 Yearbook. Washington, D. C.: Association for Supervision and Curriculum Development, NEA, 1959.

––––––. "Toward Improved Classroom Organization." *Planning and Organizing for Teaching.* Washington, D. C.: NEA Project on the Instructional Program of the Public Schools, 1963, pp. 93-118.

––––––. "Three Dimensions in Organizing the Curriculum for Learning and Teaching." In *Frontiers of Elementary Education III,* edited by Vincent J. Glennon. Syracuse, N. Y.: Syracuse University Press, 1956, pp. 11-22.

Herrick, Virgil E. *Strategies of Curriculum Development: The Works of Virgil E. Herrick.* Compiled and edited by James B. Macdonald; Dan W. Anderson, and Frank B. May. Columbus, Ohio: Charles E. Merrill Books, 1965.

Joyce, Bruce R. *Alternative Models of Elementary Education.* Waltham, Mass.: Blaisdell Publishing, 1969. Chapters 6 and 7.

Lee, Dorris M. *Diagnostic Teaching.* Washington, D. C.: Dept. of Elementary-Kindergarten-Nursery Education, NEA, 1966.

Nerbovig, Marcella. *Unit Planning: A Model for Curriculum Development.* Worthington, Ohio: Charles A. Jones Publishing, 1970.

Raths, Louis et al. *Values and Teaching.* Columbus, Ohio: Charles E. Merrill Books, 1966.

Taba, Hilda. *Teaching Strategies and Cognitive Functioning in Elementary School Children.* San Francisco: San Francisco State College, 1966.

IV. References for Classroom Personnel (*See* page 131)

Deutsch, Martin et al. *The Disadvantaged Child.* New York: Basic Books, 1968.

Flanders, Ned. A., and Simon, A. "Teacher Effectiveness." In *Encyclopedia of Educational Research.* New York: Macmillan, 1969, pp. 1423-37.

Fox, Robert et al. *Diagnosing Learning Environments.* Chicago: Science Research Associates, 1966.

Goodlad, John I. "Toward Improved Personnel, Resources, Time, and Space Organization." *Planning and Organizing for Teaching.* Washington, D. C.: NEA Project on the Instructional Program of the Public Schools, 1963, pp. 119-38.

Jackson, Philip W. *Life in Classrooms.* New York: Holt, Rinehart & Winston, 1968.

Smith, Louis M., and Geoffrey, William. *The Complexities of an Urban Classroom.* New York: Holt, Rinehart & Winston, 1968.

*See also* page 138 for References listed for Part One: School Information, IV. School Personnel

V. References for Materials and Equipment in Evidence (*See* page 132)

Association for Childhood Education International. *Bits and Pieces: Imaginative Uses for Children's Learning.* Washington, D. C.: The Association, 1967.

————. *Involvement Bulletin Boards.* Washington, D. C.: The Association, 1970.

Gerlach, Vernon S., and Ely, Donald P. *Teaching and Media: A Systematic Approach.* Englewood Cliffs, N. J.: Prentice-Hall, 1971.

Haney, John B., and Ulmer, Eldon J. *Educational Media and the Teacher.* Dubuque, Iowa: William C. Brown Co., 1970.

*See also* page 140 for References listed for Part One: School Information, V. Resources

VI. References for Instruction (*See* page 133)

Armstrong, Robert J.; Cornell, Terry; Kraner, Robert E.; and Roberson, E. Wayne. *The Development and Evaluation of Behavioral Objectives.* Worthington, Ohio: Charles A. Jones Publishing, 1970.

Association for Supervision and Curriculum Development, NEA. *Evaluation as Feedback and Guide.* 1967 Yearbook. Washington, D. C.: The Association, 1967.

Bloom, Benjamin S., ed. *Taxonomy of Educational Objectives: Cognitive Domain.* New York: Longmans, Green & Co., 1956.

Bower, Eli M., and Hollister, William G., eds. *Behavioral Science Frontiers in Education.* New York: John Wiley & Sons, 1967.

Howes, Virgil M. *Individualization of Instruction: A Teaching Strategy.* New York: Macmillan, 1970.

Hunter, Madeline. "Individualized Instruction. *Instructor* (March, 1970), pp. 53-63.

Joyce, Bruce R., and Harootunian, Berj. *The Structure of Teaching.* Chicago: Science Research Associates, 1967.

Krathwohl, David R.; Bloom, Benjamin S.; and Masia, Bertram B. *Taxonomy of Educational Objectives: Affective Domain.* New York: David McKay Co., 1964.

Simpson, Elizabeth Jane. "The Classification of Educational Objectives, Psychomotor Domain," *Illinois Teacher of Home Economics* X (Winter, 1966-67): 110-44.

VII. References for Classroom Climate and Interaction Patterns (*See* page 133)

Borton, Terry. *Reach, Touch and Teach: Student Concern and Process Education.* New York: McGraw-Hill Book Co., 1970.

Brown, George I. *Human Teaching for Human Learning: An Introduction to Confluent Education.* New York: Viking Press, 1971.

Dennison, George. *The Lives of Children.* New York: Random House, 1969.

Flanders, Ned A. *Interaction Analysis in the Classroom: A Manual for Observers.* Ann Arbor, Mich.: University of Michigan, 1966.

Fox, Robert et al. *Diagnosing Classroom Learning Environments.* Chicago: Science Research Associates, 1966.

Hitt, William D. *Education as a Human Enterprise.* Worthington, Ohio: Charles A. Jones Publishing, 1973.

Moustakas, Clark. *The Authentic Teacher: Sensitivity and Awareness in the Classroom.* Cambridge, Mass.: Howard A. Doyle Publishing Co., 1966.

Rich, John Martin. *Humanistic Foundations of Education.* Worthington, Ohio: Charles A. Jones Publishing, 1971.

Richardson, Elizabeth. *The Environment of Learning: Conflict and Understanding in the Secondary School.* New York: Weybright and Talley, 1967.

Rogers, Carl. *Freedom to Learn.* Columbus, Ohio: Charles E. Merrill Books, 1969.

Sears, Pauline S., and Sherman, V. S. *In Pursuit of Self-Esteem.* Belmont, Calif.: Wadsworth Publishing Co., 1964.

Simon, Anita, and Boyer, E. G. I., eds. *Mirrors for Behavior; an Anthology of Classroom Observation Instruments.* Philadelphia: Research for Better Schools, 1967.

VIII. References for Significant Problems of Classroom and Attempts to Solve Them (*See* page 134)

Fuchs, Estelle. *Teachers Talk: Views from Inside City Schools.* Garden City: Doubleday Anchor Books, 1969.

Institute for Development of Educational Activities, Inc., Research Division. *The Problem Solving School.* Nine classroom booklets, three handbooks. Dayton, Ohio: /I/D/E/A/, 1972.

Schmuck, Richard; Chesler, Mark; and Lippitt, Ronald. *Problem Solving to Improve Classroom Learning.* Chicago: Science Research Associates, 1966.

X. References for General Impressional Observations (*See* page 135)

Jackson, Philip W. *Life in Classrooms.* New York: Holt, Rinehart & Winston, 1968.

_____. *The Teacher and the Machine.* Horace Mann Lecture, 1967. Pittsburgh: University of Pittsburgh Press, 1968.

Smith, Louis M., and Geoffrey, William. *The Complexities of an Urban Classroom; an Analysis Toward a General Theory of Teaching.* New York: Holt, Rinehart & Winston, 1968.

# Index